THOSE
HE CAME TO SAVE

THOSE HE CAME TO SAVE

ROY C. PUTNAM

Abingdon
Nashville

Those He Came to Save

Copyright © 1978 by Roy C. Putnam

Library of Congress Cataloging in Publication Data

PUTNAM, ROY C   1928-
Those he came to save.

1.   Methodist Church—Sermons.   2.   Sermons, American.
I.   Title.
BX8333.P78T48   252'.7   77-13764

ISBN 0-687-41862-3

MANUFACTURED BY THE PARTHENON PRESS AT NASH-
VILLE, TENNESSEE, UNITED STATES OF AMERICA

To Ren and Cindy
with love

Crown him the Lord of Life,
Who triumphed o'er the grave,
And rose victorious in the strife
For those he came to save.

Matthew Bridges

CONTENTS

GOOD NEWS TO THE BRUISED

INTRODUCTION

Every four years the American people witness the spectacle of two political conventions. From these conventions we have learned to watch for and listen to the keynote addresses. These speeches will set forth the issues that are of major concern. They will strike a note that is calculated to be sounded throughout the days of campaigning.

During this time the people are challenged to discern the ablest leadership. We have come to expect that a true leader will present the people with the hard truth, call them to difficult paths to follow, and appeal to their highest qualities, not their basest instincts. A true leader will tell us what we ought to hear, not what we want to hear.

11

The false leader will cater to the prejudices and preferences of the people. He will inflame their fears, hates, angers, and resentments. He will hoodwink the people into thinking they can reconcile the irreconcilable, moralize the immoral, rationalize the unreasonable, and will promise a mock millennium during which people can enjoy the good without being good.

Few have examined the most amazing keynote address by the greatest leader of all time. It dates back to a period of notable political and social unrest. It is the address that Jesus Christ himself delivered in Nazareth. One day he laid aside his carpenter's tools and went into a little synagogue in his hometown and announced a manifesto (Luke 4:16–20).

"The spirit of the Lord God is upon me; because the Lord hath anointed me to preach good tidings unto the meek; he hath sent me to bind up the broken-hearted, to proclaim liberty to the captives, and the opening of the prison to them that are bound; To proclaim the acceptable year of the Lord" (Isa. 61:1–2). It is awe-inspiring to read it for the first time and see where Jesus stopped. He put a period where Isaiah put a comma. Isaiah went on to say "and the day of vengeance of our God." But Jesus is saying in effect: "I am going to fulfill scripture by ushering in a new day. I am going to interpose a new dispensation. It will be the day of grace. I am going to push back the day of vengeance. It will come; but not now. 'Now' will be the day of salvation."

12

With the death of Jesus an old order ended. With the Resurrection a new order began. The central claim of the New Testament is the announcement of the birth of a new world and a new humanity. This is why Jesus is arrestingly called the last Adam (I Cor. 15:45). *Adam* means history. A new history begins with the raising of Jesus from the dead. G. K. Chesterton describes it in this way:

> On the third day the friends of Christ coming at daybreak to the place found the grave empty and the stone rolled away. In varying ways they realized the new wonder; but even they hardly realized that the world had died in the night. What they were looking at was the first day of a new creation, with a new heaven and a new earth; and in a semblance of the gardener God walked again in the garden, in the cool, not of the evening, but of the dawn.

Jesus was announcing a new day. This day of salvation to which Jesus referred was known as the "year of jubilee." It was a most extraordinary arrangement, as described in Leviticus 25. It was the final year in a cycle of fifty years, the culmination of a rhythm of sabbath years. It was ushered in by the priest's blowing of the ram's horn (trumpet) to proclaim liberty for the oppressed.

So now an otherwise bleak future full of grinding despair could be suddenly flushed with hope. That was his mission in Nazareth. He was announcing the commencement of the celebration of this unbelievable year. It would affect the whole of their lives. It meant a spiritual release and perception that would have its outworking in the total life of the people—socially, politically, economically, and ecologically.

Not only did Christ minister to all classes of people in his day, but because he is alive and working in and through his church today, the good news can be trumpeted to people found within this complete category of human need. The bankrupt, the brokenhearted, the bound, the blind, the bruised, constitute those he came to save.

GOOD NEWS
TO THE BANKRUPT

The Spirit of the Lord is upon me, because he hath
anointed me to preach the gospel to the poor.
(Luke 4:18)

THE NATURE OF OUR DEBT

New York City's declaration of bankruptcy in 1975
flashed a warning of fiscal irresponsibility to the
nation. We can make a simple deduction: there is
no place in creation for nonproducers. There is no
life without generators. When consumers con-
sume producers, bankruptcy is inevitable. The
result is a New York City, which is a prototype of
mid-century man's dilemma. Paul Rees describes
our bankrupt sophistication:

New York City! With a higher skyline than any city
on the planet! With amusement enough to make
every day a Roman Holiday and boredom enough to
keep the world's biggest concentration of psychia-
trists busy round the clock. With culture smooth

15

enough to please an Athenian and corruption enough to blanch a Judas! With people enough to start a nation and resentments and hatreds enough to start a war! With din in her ears and speed in her blood and sweat on her face and guilt on her soul and the 'Unknown God' in her nebulous longings.

Guilt on her soul! That constitutes the real bank-ruptcy of our century. That means not simply being poor but having demands made upon us that we cannot meet. This is precisely man's con-dition.

I

Jesus came to save the bankrupt, to show how his mercy outdistances our gratitude by leaps and bounds. Jesus tells the story of the two debtors (see Matt. 18:21). The parable introduces us to an executive who had absconded funds from the royal Exchequer. An audit revealed that he had taken 10,000 talents—an exorbitant amount. (The combined annual taxes of Judea, Idumea, Samaria, Galilee, and Perea amounted to only 800 talents.) This embezzlement created such a furor in the royal court as to bring down upon the dis-honest man the full weight of the king's wrath. Justice demanded this guilty embezzler be "sold, and his wife, and children, and all that he had, and payment to be made. The servant therefore fell down, and worshipped him saying, Lord, have patience with me, and I will pay thee all. Then the Lord of that servant was moved with compassion, and loosed him, and forgave him the debt" (vv. 25–27). This extravagant pardon stretches the imagination of the most incredulous thinker. Indeed, it was a king's pardon.

> Thou art coming to a king,
> Large petitions with thee bring,
> For his grace and power are such
> None can ever ask too much.
>
> John Newton

Of course, the punch line of this parable is that such grace can never flow into us until we have the same disposition toward others, enabling this blessed beneficence to flow outward. For God's love is like electricity; it never will go in where it cannot get out.

But there is in this parable not only the major key of God's forgiving grace but the minor key of our indebtedness. For a commentary on this we turn to the inspired apostle Paul, Christ's finest interpreter.

II

In building his framework of Christian theology, Paul insists that not only has man sinned in falling short of God's standard, but he has fallen below his own standard— "the good that I would I do not" (Rom. 7:19). Not only has man become unlike God, but he has come to hate Him— "the carnal mind is enmity against God" (Rom. 8:7). Not only has he left his Father's house, but he thinks that to live at home in the will of God is a bad thing for him. Not only has he spent all his substance, but he has incurred an indebtedness that shadows him wherever he goes. And he has no resources with which to cancel the debts.

What is the nature of this indebtedness? When we run a red traffic light, we may pay a fine and square the record. But what if we speak a word that wounds a child and warps his character? Or suppose by another word we damage another's reputation. Or suppose we break a trust so that never again can that confidence in our fidelity be replaced in the mind of a friend, unsoiled, unsullied, untarnished. When love is betrayed, how will we atone for that?

The Hebrews believed that any moral transgression had reality. When one spoke a word one created something as real as a stone or a tree or a star. That is why Jesus said, "By thy words, thou shalt be justified, and by thy words thou shalt be condemned" (Matt. 12:37). Suppose that we speak an unkind word or a word of evil intent to debase another. Every time we meet, we have to face that person and the word we have spoken. It hangs there heavily in the very matrix of our relationship. Words affect us far more drastically than do material possessions. When we speak we bring to life an entity for good or for evil. And sin is there. It cannot be spoken away. It must be borne away. The Hebrew word for forgiveness is the same for "borne." "Blessed is the man whose sin is forgiven" literally means "blessed is the man whose sin is borne." "Surely he hath borne our griefs,

18

and carried our sorrows" (Isa. 53:4). As a pastor I work with sin every day but do not have to deal with it. God had to deal with it. That is the reason he said to his disciples before going to the Cross, "Whither I go, thou canst not follow me now; but thou shalt follow me afterwards" (John 13:36). We can follow afterward because Christ has dealt with our sin which produces guilt.

Guilt has beclouded the spirit of modern man. All our attempts to redress the wrongs of life and to pay our debts find us up against an incalculable poverty that is overshadowed by the debt of our past. We have contracted an eternal debt, and there are no mere human means to pay it.

No earnestness of intention to do better next time can ever suffice for the agonizing awareness that the past bears a stain that is indelible and a wrong that is irreversible. This awareness is heightened by that inexorable announcement in Ecclesiastes 3:15, "God requireth that which is past."

The past is never something from which we can divorce ourselves. It belongs to us. We are our past. It is the mark and evidence of our revolt against God. The past colors the present, and its disquieting shadow is cast across our tomorrows. Paul calls it "the handwriting against us." "Fear hath torment," says John. We fear because instinctively we know that in the end we will be accountable. "Give an account of thy stewardship; for thou mayest be no longer steward" (Luke 16:2).

19

We know that our past will outrun us into the future, and there the finger of justice will be pointed to us saying, "Thou art the man!"

This constitutes our dilemma. It is no accident that in an age when theology is at such a discount, our hospitals are full of psychotics, neurotics, and chaotics! It bears full witness to the fact of man's total inadequacy to rid himself of the guilt of the past, to master the circumstances of the present, and to meet the exigencies of the future.

III

It is wonderful to know that we can reckon *on* God. It is terrible to think that we have to reckon *with* God. When that dawns upon us we seek escape. The stillness comes alive with God. That accounts for the noise and countless distractions we have brought to the fore to drown out the intolerable voice that speaks within us. Our bankruptcy can be traced through all the cultural forms—our art, music, drama, dance, philosophy, and literature. It is the guilt of the soul, clothing itself in all sorts of strange expressions, which psychologists call dissociated symptoms.

We do not give these symptoms over to theological categories. But all the dissatisfactions that plague us can be traced to our spiritual bankruptcy.

We are poor because we are under a depression constituted by our sins. A sinner in the biblical frame of reference is one who is missing the mark. God has set a high mark of destiny for us. Scottish novelist and poet George MacDonald said, "Never suspecting what a noble creature he was meant to be, he never saw what a poor creature he was." We are experiencing the disparity of what we are and what we were called to be. That produces guilt, anxiety, and frustration. A soul discontent with itself will soon spread discontent outside itself. If we are not serving one another, we will soon burden one another. Our personal self-hate becomes hate of others. Communism uses this for capital in its philosophy of class struggle. There is in this system a special affinity for souls who are already having inner turmoil. So a whole economic system is built on this human foible. Associated with this inner conflict is a tendency to become hypercritical. Unhappy people always blame somebody else or some system for their miseries.

This is basic in our understanding of the good news to the bankrupt. For the anxiety complex lies here; it does not emanate from our animal origin. Animals, left to themselves, never have anxieties. Birds do not develop a psychosis about whether they should migrate in winter. A hippopotamus never asks rhetorical questions. He just rolls in the mud and sings:

> Mud, mud, glorious mud,
> Nothing quite like it
> For cooling the blood.

21

But try as we might to be mud-oriented, we cannot be content. It takes eternity in the heart to make us despair. Nikolia Berdyaev's dictum stands: "Where there is no God there is no man." God created us to live on the illimitable resources of "Christ in us the hope of glory." Therefore Paul could say in II Corinthians 2:14, "Now thanks be unto God, which always causeth us to triumph in Christ." But no sooner had he made that mighty asseveration than the poverty of his soul was exposed. Christ's call is to triumphant living. But, alas, we know our poor hearts too well. This is not our experience. There is a dichotomy between our call and our condition. We are like the track star who was a high jumper. The coach put the bar to the highest possible notch. The jumper looked at it and said, "Coach, how can I ever jump that high?" "I'll tell you how," replied the coach. "Just throw your heart over that bar first, and the rest is sure to follow!"

God raised the bar of our humanity to the highest possible notch when he gave us Jesus. We find that Jesus Christ only accentuates our bankruptcy. The inarticulate cry of humanity is, Who is sufficient for these things? Few there are who go on to find the answer that Paul enunciated in II Corinthians 3:5, "Not that we are sufficient of ourselves to think any thing as of ourselves; but our sufficiency is of God."

If we look at Christ, throw our heart away to him, the rest is sure to follow. But if we cling to what we have—our selfishness, our sickness, our autonomy—we thus cut off the source of forgiving grace, healing power, and abundant supply that God wants to flow to us and through us. The principle of faith is that we relinquish what we have, and he releases in us what he is. "Be careful [anxious] for nothing; but in every thing by prayer and supplication with thanksgiving let your requests be made known unto God" (Phil. 4:6).

Thus we learn to expose every need, however large; every horizon, however dark; every problem, however threatening—expose all to the Lord Jesus Christ, stand back, and say, "Thank you!" For our sufficiency is of God.

WHO, THEN, CAN BE SAVED?

One thing thou lackest.
Mark 10:21

It has always been a mixed company that hedges about Christ. Yet there is one thing they all have in common—a consciousness of their bankruptcy. Whether they be kings or commoners, princes or paupers, saints or sages—in the presence of Jesus Christ they are all forced to cry out, "What lack I yet?"

Jesus and a young ruling aristocrat were mutually attracted to each other. The perfection of Jesus and the potential of the young man were juxtaposed. There was no doubt about his enthusiasm for life. He ran to Jesus. Drab conventional security was not enough. Dull tedious conformity to social mores did not satisfy. There was an awful sense of bankruptcy in terms of "heaven's treasures." He desired something that the edge of time could not diminish. He longed for the import of a vital pledge to the heart that the bleak shadows of circumstances could not drain away. There must have been a keen perception that Jesus had the answer to the deeper quest of his soul. So he came, with grand credentials.

Certainly he did not lack *health of body*. He came "running and kneeled to him." His were not knees stiffened with arthritis. There was the surge of health and the suppleness of youth in them. This is greatly to be desired. It was never the Christian, but the gnostic who said that the body is evil. The development of medicine is concommitant with the ascendance of the Christian faith in any culture. The Christian Church has always put a great premium on the human body. It has never doubted that God is on the side of health. The church acknowledges the presence of sickness and physical disability but at the same time affirms God's working with us, whether by prayer or medical skill and facility, to recover health. The church anticipates a world where sickness and death will be swept away forever. The Christian prays confidently, "Heal me according to thy will, that I may enjoy and profess on earth what is enjoyed and realized in heaven." Health abounded in this young man. Jesus must have loved him for the strength of his youth. So it was not infirmity or age that drove him to Jesus.

Neither did he lack *intellectual honesty*. He asked the ultimate question: "What shall I do that

I may inherit eternal life?" It was a personal query-ing of a mind that had been grappling with eternal issues. He did not belong to the cult of mindless-ness that is everywhere on the increase today. He sought that which would objectively satisfy his desire for truth. He knew there was an authorita-tive path that would steer his thinking accurately.

This is an important detail. We are surfeited today with subjective speculation. However, the heart cannot embrace what the mind cannot ap-prove. A man said to Rufus Jones, the Quaker, "When I come to church I feel like unscrewing my head and placing it under the seat, because in our religious meetings I never have any use for any-thing above the collar button." We need the warn-ing of Bishop Handley Moule, "Beware of un-theological devotion and undevotional theology." Paul spoke of those in his day who had "a zeal without knowledge." Christ loves intellectual in-tegrity: "Worship the Lord with all your mind," he once enjoined.

Nor did this young ruler lack a *thirsting heart.* He gave positive reciprocation to the secret draw-ing of God. He was enacting the warm feeling stated in the Forty-second Psalm: "As the hart panteth after the water brooks, so panteth my soul after thee, O God" (v. 1). He had come from a landed family. He was raised to be a popular leader. He knew the power of money. But there walked among him and his contemporaries a man whose dignity and moral power exposed the pov-erty of the aristocrat's own soul. This master in

Israel longed for the mastery he saw in Jesus Christ. The desire for authentic living seized him. A bird is perfectly content with walking on two legs until it discovers it has wings.

He did not lack *social consciousness*. "And Jesus said unto him, . . . Thou knowest the commandments. . . . And he answered and said unto him, Master, all these have I observed from my youth" (Mark 10:18-20). These commandments had to do with man's relationship with man.

We should note that two distinct obligations are laid upon us by Jesus. One is vertical and the other horizontal. When we "give a cup of cold water" (horizontal), it is to be given "in Jesus' name" (vertical). The ultimate tragedy of life is not social or economic or political inequity. It is, rather, a person who fails to know who and why he or she is and to have upon him or her the high calling of God in Christ Jesus.

Service to neighbor is not the same as love for God. They are inseparable but not identical. That is why the rich young ruler could keep the commandments while resisting God's love. Karl Barth once commented, "The fact that the source must and does become a river does not mean that the source is not something true and distinctive as opposed to the river. Indeed, without this true and distinctive thing which we call the source there could be no river." In other words, all who love will serve, but not all service springs from love. We would say, "All citizens of North Carolina are Americans, but not all Americans are citizens of North Carolina." The commandments are not interchangeable. This young man had kept the commandments. Yet keeping the commandments can be less an expression of faith than a substitute for faith. The bad man's sin cannot bring satisfaction to life, but neither can the good man's self-righteousness.

Thus, the rich young ruler did not lack health of body, integrity of mind, intensity of heart, or sensitivity to social need. Yet, he was not satisfied that he had received that quality of life that is eternal. So he went away sorrowful. Rich in materialism, correct in deportment, honest in intellect, he was bankrupt of satisfaction.

Where did he lack? The clue is "Then Jesus beholding him loved him" (Mark 10:21). That fact was his opportunity both for salvation and for consternation. Have you ever been loved by the wrong person? That is, did you ever wish to be loved not so much by a particular person because you were not yet ready to reciprocate that love? It is a terrible thing to be loved by God, for that love is a consuming fire. It is so amazing and so divine as to demand our souls, our lives, our all. And that fire was too hot, that love too consuming for this young man. Augustine once said, "One loving heart sets another on fire!" The ruler in Israel was not ready to say with Amy Carmichael:

> Give me the love that leads the way,
> The faith that nothing can dismay,
> The hope no disappointments tire,
> The passion that will burn like fire.

28

Let me not sink to be a clod,
Make me thy fuel, Flame of God.

"Go thy way, sell whatsoever thou hast, and
give to the poor, and thou shalt have treasure in
heaven: and come, take up the cross, and follow
me" (v. 21). He had been giving to the poor, else he
could not have kept the commandments. But his
heart awaited the revelation of inward motivation.
Revelation 3:21 describes Christ standing at the
door of man's heart, wanting to come in to feed the
springs of life. Scholar John Stott suggests that while
He stands at the door and knocks "we keep repeating our prayers through the keyhole and continue
shoving our money under the doorsill." What God
really desires is that we open the door and allow him
to be the Head of our house, the Life of our living,
the Love that sanctifies our loving, and the Joy of our
hearts.

"Taking up the cross" was not Christ's way of
saying that a man is to give up everything. The
proposition is to give up *the right* to everything.
This young man had mastered the art of investment. Jesus was teaching him the art of divest-
ment. "How hardly shall they that have riches
enter into the kingdom of God!" (v. 23). Possessions have a way of making us love them, trust
and serve them. How difficult to trust in Christ
when we have so much wealth, success, and
status to which we may cling. All these things are
so demanding. "How hard is it for them that trust
in riches to enter into the kingdom of God!" (v.

29

24). The operative word here is *trust*. How hard it is to trust not in those riches nor to allow them to offer us false security and satisfaction. When materialism becomes focal, then spiritual things become peripheral.

But how hard it is for us to capitulate to the lordship of Christ until we repudiate the claim of mammon upon us. That is the reason Jesus said, "It is hard to enter the kingdom," because the Kingdom means assessment of the authority and worthiness of Jesus Christ. It elicits total, utter, loving dependence upon him as the source of our supply. And the young artistocrat had found supreme worth in another object.

Jesus comments, "It is easier for a camel to go through the eye of a needle, than for a rich man to enter into the kingdom of God" (v. 25). Attempts can be made to modify that statement; but we must at times face the enigma of scripture and defy simplistic proof texts and dialectical conundrums. This is simply Jesus' way of saying that it is impossible!

The disciples were confounded. No wonder they were "astonished out of measure, saying among themselves, Who then can be saved?" (v. 26). They were saying in effect, "If a kid like this can't make it, who of us ought to try?"

Then comes the incisive word: "the things that are impossible with men are possible with God." Put that over against the lostness of our day, the overwhelming odds that mount against the church, and the incorrigibility of human nature.

The announcement in Nazareth on that sabbath day long ago echoes across the ages: "Good news to the poor!" I know it is conjecture at best. But many have been the surmisings that this young man later realized how poor he was in the midst of his riches and then joined the apostolic band. There is this vignette in the book of Acts: "as many as were possessors of lands or houses sold them, and brought the prices of the things that were sold, and laid them down at the apostles' feet: and distribution was made unto every man according as he had need" (4:34).

Could this young man have been Barnabas? The things that are impossible with men are possible with God! "For ye see your calling, brethren, how that not many wise men after the flesh, not many mighty, not many noble, are called: but God has chosen the foolish things of the world to confound the wise " (I Cor. 1:26–27).

The Countess of Huntingdon was caught up in the early Methodist movement. She was a friend of Whitefield's and Wesley's and gave them much financial support. She testified that she was saved because of one word. "Not *many* noble are called," she said, "yet it does not read that not *any* noble are called."

I would like to think of just such a blessed exception with regard to the rich young ruler. "Jesus beholding him, loved him." Love never fails. That is the good news of the gospel. That love stands on the doorsill of our indecision and knocks. We are preoccupied with building our Babylons. We shore up our affluence and think we are secure behind our little mental Maginot Lines. But the consummate wisdom of man cannot meet man's deepest need nor satisfy his highest aspiration.

Paul went to the cultural center of the known world at the behest of that man who cried, "Come over into Macedonia, and help us" (Acts 16:9). Here was the world's center of learning, epitomized in their sciences and arts. Yet dire poverty lay at the heart of all their culture. Hence the call, "Come over . . . and help us." The next verse is revealing: "Immediately we endeavoured to go into Macedonia, assuredly gathering that the Lord had called us for to preach the gospel unto them" (16:10).

That same cry comes today through our journalism, drama, philosophy, and music—What lack I yet? To this generation the significance of the words of Jesus fairly leap into relevancy, "The Spirit of the Lord is upon me, . . . to preach the gospel to the poor" (Luke 4:18).

If man will not find in Christ the answer to his bankruptcy, the satisfaction for hunger, the inspiration for living, the freedom from slavery, then in all the vast reaches of this unending universe, he shall perpetuate his poverty forever. Only in Christ will there be fulfilled the prophecy: "The expectation of the poor shall not perish for ever" (Ps. 9:18).

FAILURE IS NOT FOREVER

But we trusted that it had been he
which should have redeemed Israel.
Luke 24:21

There never was a more hopeless situation facing
any people than what faced the disciples of Jesus
when he died and was buried. They saw mass
opinion release a beast in Barabbas and slay the
best in Christ. They saw human iniquity nail justice to a tree. They saw goodness flung backward
in its forward march, beaten and broken, white
and still in death. They watched as a confederacy
of lies carried truth to the grave to rot.

No wonder despair gripped their hearts.
Perplexity battered and beseiged their minds.
Their dearest hopes came crashing down in ruin.
And they were facing the ultimate doubt—that
God himself is indifferent and impotent in the

33

face of arrogant evil. Listen to the pathos of their words: "But we trusted that it had been he which should have redeemed Israel: and beside all this, to-day is the third day since these things were done" (Luke 24:21).

Bankrupt Hopes

Three things characterize the disciples' destitute situation. First, we are told that their eyes were *shut:* "But their eyes were holden that they should not know him" (Luke 24:16). Paul, in writing to the Ephesian Christians, commended them for their faith and love, but then went on to pray for them to have "the eyes of [their] understanding enlightened," to know "the hope of his calling, . . . the riches of the glory of his inheritance in the saints, and . . . the exceeding greatness of his power to us-ward who believe" (see Eph. 1:15–19).

The bankruptcy of hope can be traced to eyes that have shut out the vision of Christ's inestimable victory. The message of the gospel is that Christ died for us and rose again to live in us. Every true believer has in himself the illimitable resources of Christ. There is no such thing as a believer who does not have the Holy Spirit living in him. That is either the driest piece of theology we could ever hear, or it is the most audacious and exciting truth we should ever face.

Second, we are told that not only were the disci-

34

ples' eyes shut, but their faces were *sad*. "And he said unto them, What manner of communications are these that ye have one to another, as ye walk, and are sad?" (v. 17). This is largely the disposition of the church today. Our deadpan faces prefigure a twentieth-century Christianity that is emasculated of its exuberant song and its triumphant march.

We look at the circumstances around us and surmise that God has failed. After the disciples had gone out preaching the kingdom of God, Jesus said to them, "I saw Satan fall like lightning from heaven" (Luke 10:18 RSV). Sure, publicans still kept crooked tax records, muggers still lurked along the road from Jerusalem to Jericho, slaves remained the property of their masters, and Rome still appeared to dominate history with an iron hand. But Jesus saw in the preaching of the gospel sign enough that evil was defeated. We still think, however, that it is God who has fallen from heaven, not Satan. The church today is obsessed with a defeatist mentality. We examine and assess and lament our statistics and mull over our reports and reason and explain our defeat. All the while our risen and regnant Lord draws near to us. "Rejoice in the Lord alway. . . . Let your moderation be known unto all men. The Lord is at hand" (Phil. 4:4–5). A more accurate translation would render "The Lord is at your elbow!" Thank God, Jesus drew near to counsel them. He never left them with their own analysis of the human situation.

35

Not only were their eyes *shut* and their faces *sad*, but third, we are told that their hearts were *slow*. "Then he said unto them, O fools, and slow of heart to believe all that the prophets have spoken" (Luke 24:25). This is a condition with which we are all familiar. It is a paralysis of the soul. We are keen on many subjects, alert about social issues and in political palaver. But we are so obtuse when it comes to spiritual matters. We can have unlimited conversation on any number of subjects. Then we retire to our knees to talk with God, and suddenly we are tongue-tied and extremely weary.

It takes more than birth and inertia to be a Christian. There must be a desire to "grasp that purpose for which Christ Jesus grasped me" (Phil. 3:12 Phillips). The disciples' problem was that they were communing and reasoning among themselves (v. 15) when they should have been believing the scriptures. Why is it that we are so quick to lay hold upon the current philosophies of men and so slow to believe the Word of God? Why are we so quick to read *The Secular City* and so slow to read *The City of God?* Why are we so prone to accept as authoritative the speculations of some learned man and so slow to admit that "God is true and every man a liar"?

We simply have not discovered what God is after in history. So we get on our panels and amass our confusion and organize our indefiniteness. The wag who described a panel discussion as the "place where we pool our ignorance" was not wide of the mark. "O fools, and slow of heart to believe all that the prophets have spoken!"

Blessed Hands

"And it came to pass, as he sat at meat with them, he took bread, and blessed it, and brake, and gave to them. And their eyes were opened, and they knew him. . . . And they told . . . how he was known of them in breaking of bread" (Luke 24:30–31, 35).

They sat at meat with him. Those livid scars received from the cosmic campaign fought at Calvary suddenly glowed with meaning. "And their eyes were opened, and they knew him." Christ had died to acquit them and had risen to accept them.

Those hands communicated something words could never do. No wonder Luke makes a particular point of it: "He shewed them his hands" (24:40). There is a very interesting communication that can be observed in American sports. When a player has scored a certain victory, such as a touchdown in football, he hastens toward his teammates, takes both hands, and slaps them against the hands of his teammates—sharing his victory celebration with them.

Something like this happened as the disciples felt the impact of those hands on their human spirits. It was as though Christ had transferred such a victory to them that their hands began to quiver with power, and their eyes were ravished with delight.

They were eating bread broken by those hands that bore the mark of redemption. He had said to them just a few days earlier, "I will not any more eat thereof, until it be fulfilled in the kingdom of God" (Luke 22:16). Before Christ rose they faced the sepulcher. They were despair-oriented. That is symbolic of the human race. Our deep, secret psychology is conditioned by the knowledge that we are in an endless procession toward death. But since Jesus rose again, a deeper knowledge possesses us. We face away from the tomb. We are life-oriented. "I am the living bread which came down from heaven. . . . He that eateth of this bread shall live for ever" (John 6:51, 58).

These disciples knew that all the arrogant might of Rome and all the sinister powers of hell could not stop Christ. He would outlast the centuries. Death no more held ultimate power over them, for it had no dominion over him. Everything they thought had been closed was now wide open. And here was a tiny, disillusioned group of people, possessed with their own resentfulness, torn by their own fearfulness, sequestered in their own carefulness. They weren't invading society. They were more concerned that society didn't invade them.

And then suddenly Jesus joined them. Luke makes the point that "Jesus drew near and went with them." Until Jesus joined them, a remnant of a church was operating in all the frustration of fear, friction, and failure. Suddenly they caught a vision of the risen Christ. It turned their sorrow to shouting, their tribulation into testimony, and their night of despondency into the dawn of an eternal morning. Failure was not forever.

Everything shifted from a natural to a spiritual perspective. They saw the other side of things. And when they did, it made all previous reasoning foolish. They had gone in broad daylight, but it had grown dark. They returned at night, but it had become light. The day and night are just parables. With confused minds and cold hearts their outward journey to Emmaus was gloomy. But their inward journey back was with burning heart, enlightened mind, and radiant testimony.

That's what happens when Jesus joins the church, opens the scripture, and sets us down at his banquet table. In Psalm 105:37 we have a commentary on the Passover when Israel was led out of Egypt. It is symbolic of what was happening to these disciples after the Resurrection as they were delivered out of their bondage. "He brought them forth also with silver and gold: and there was not one feeble person among their tribes." What a miracle! Two and one-quarter million people, young and old, given strength for the journey.

> Strengthen the wavering lines,
> 'Stablish, continue our march,
> On, to the bound of the waste,
> On, to the city of God.
> Matthew Arnold

Strength for the journey was given them because the blood had been applied but also because the Lamb had been eaten. That strength is available today through the Lord's Supper, as Jesus joins us to serve us with his own adequacy. "He was known of them in breaking of bread" (Luke 24:35).

Burning Hearts

"And they said one to another, Did not our heart burn within us, while he talked with us by the way, and while he opened to us the scriptures?" (Luke 24:32).

To say that hope was restored is an understatement. Hope rushed back so and took possession of them that they became the avant-garde of a movement that launched Christianity upon the world like a thunderbolt and called the church into being and sent it marching in healing mercy down the centuries, "fair as the moon, clear as the sun, and terrible as any army with banners" (Song of Sol. 6:10).

Their hearts fairly burned with assurance. Without even unpacking, they went back to the city, back to the scene of conflict, back to the place of apparent disaster and defeat. They did not merely stand in the world and bear witness of the risen Christ. They stood in the power of a risen Christ and bore witness to the world.

What made those hearts burn? "While he talked with us by the way, and while he opened to us the scriptures" (Luke 24:32). It was the result of seeing

Jesus in the scriptures; communion with the living Christ and the opening of the Word.

THE INFALLIBLE STATUS OF THE WORD. Jesus accepted the written revelation without equivocation. Here is the major reason evangelical believers accept the Bible as God's Word written, inspired by the Holy Spirit, and authoritative over their lives. John Stott says:

> It is not that we take a blindfold leap into the darkness and resolve to believe what we strongly suspect is incredible. Nor is it because the universal church consistently taught this for the first eighteen centuries of its life (though it did, and this long tradition is not to be lightly set aside). Nor is it because God's Word authenticates itself to us as we read it today— by the majesty of its themes, by the unity of its message and by the power of its influence. No. The overriding reason for accepting the divine inspiration and authority of Scripture is plain loyalty to Jesus.

The central issue relates, therefore, not to the authority of the Bible but to the authority of Christ. To reject the authority of either the Old Testament or the New Testament is to reject the authority of Christ. It is because we are determined to submit to the authority of Jesus Christ as Lord that we submit to the authority of scripture.

THE INDISPENSABLE SEARCHER OF THE WORD. "He opened to them the scriptures." He who inspired the Word now opens their minds to it. And the Word comes alive with meaning.

41

Without the quickening and confirming grace of his Presence accompanying the communication of the Word, theological truth can be information and nothing more. "It is not the night that kills, but the frost." And frosty dead orthodoxy can be devastating. The words of scripture must have his breath upon them. Otherwise, truth can rattle in our eardrums, but our understanding is never affected. It takes Christ himself, in the person of the Holy Spirit, to produce a living faith and virile godliness.

THE ALL-INCLUSIVE SCOPE OF THE WORD. "And beginning at Moses and all the prophets, he expounded unto them in all the scriptures" (v. 27). What a Bible reading this must have been! He uncovered for them the profoundest insights into the Mosaic rituals. He breathed into them the depths of that love that prompted the giving of the Law. He plucked every string in the messianic harp of the law and the prophets, tracing every note in the music of full redemption.

THE INCOMPARABLE SUBJECT OF THE WORD. "He expounded unto them in all the scriptures the things concerning himself" (v. 27). Concerning himself! Jesus Christ is the fulfillment, the centerpiece, the supreme subject of the Old Testament. He rises from every page with expression or symbol or prophecy or psalm or proverb. He is the Desire of Nations who threads the Great Book as a crimson cord stitches its way through a fine tapestry. Jesus is to the Old Testament what calcium is to lime, what carbon is to diamonds, what truth is to history, what numbers are to mathematics. All its types typify him, all its symbols signify him, all its sacrifices show him; all its truths converge in him, all its beauty is embodied in him. Its songs are his sentiments, its prophecies are his pictures, its promises are his pledges, and our hearts burn within us as we walk beside him across its living pages!

Of all the bankruptcy we humans are prone to suffer, none is worse than traversing the realm of time with no knowledge of Christ as the living, burning center of all life.

Dr. William E. Sangster, that seraphic preacher at Westminster, Central Hall, London, held fast to a deep evangelical faith. A year or two before his death he contracted an illness that slowly robbed him of his power of speech. It crept upon him. His son, Paul, wrote this in his biography: "I heard my father preach the most wonderful sermons I've ever heard in my life. But I never heard him preach like the last three months of his life when he couldn't whisper a word. It was beautiful to see his lovely, radiant, peaceful, trusting life when he knew he was running to the end." On his last Easter morning, he wrote to his daughter who was a missionary in India: "Margaret, what a dreadful thing to wake up on Easter morning and have no voice with which to shout, 'He is risen!' But how far more awful to have a voice and not want to shout it!"

Herein lies the great bankruptcy of mankind. It is not the bitter tragedies that happen *to* us that defoliate life. Rather it is what fails to happen *in* us—the release of Christ's mastery and adequacy and victory.

GOOD NEWS
TO THE BROKENHEARTED

The Spirit of the Lord is upon me, . . .
he hath sent me to heal the brokenhearted.
Luke 4:18

DEFEAT THAT FACES THE DAWN

Luke 5, John 13, John 21

In Luke 5 we have one of the most scenic descriptions in scripture. The setting is Lake of Gennesaret, along the northern shore of Galilee. Off to one side, a gaunt Galilean busily engages in the art of teaching the multitudes. In the distance, two ships float at anchor on the shifting tides. On the farther side, two fishermen clean their nets. Expletives can be heard ringing from the fishermen as they charge the atmosphere with their disdain. A long hard night of plying their trade in the waters of Galilee has yielded no compensation.

All the while, there are crowds pressing upon Jesus, the Master Teacher. He is backed right up to the water's edge. He turns to the fishermen and asks permission to use their boat as his pulpit. Here is a picturesque passage. Jesus stands in the fishing vessel to dispense the wonderful words of life. Feeling indebtedness to the fishermen from whom he has commandeered the boat, he turns to Peter. Jesus suggests that they move out to the water's depths and let down the nets for a draft of fish.

Surely Peter's mind was boggled. These were men of expertise in their field. They were scientists of the sea. They knew every inch of that water. They knew that fish were not to be found in that area of the sea at that time of day. There was no doubt about it. Those fish in Lake Tiberius were under strict orders from the Lord of all creation. At the command of Christ, they had cautiously avoided those nets. They were not about to disobey divine orders.

But the disciples remonstrated with the Lord. Peter explains, "We've scanned these waters all night and caught nothing." Little did Peter realize that there were secrets in those waters that his mind could never fathom.

Christ's timing is incredible. All things cohere in him. Thus at the propitious moment, the fish converge on those nets, straining them to the breaking point. As they are hauled aboard, the vessel sags almost to the gunwale with overflowing blessings. No doubt the disciples were given a flash of insight into one of the principles that would be reiterated throughout the Lord's ministry. *There is no such thing as success or failure. There is only obedience or disobedience to the divine Word.*

When Peter saw with what authority the Master Teacher moved, he was transfixed. Here was a man unlike any other he had ever encountered. And the appalling reality came to him. Peter himself was so unlike Jesus that it was frightening. He knew that Christ and he did not belong in the same boat. The majesty and sheer transcendence broke Peter's self-sufficiency. The effect was salutary. It elicited the first recorded prayer Peter ever uttered: "Depart from me; for I am a sinful man, O Lord" (Luke 5:8).

Then came Christ's prophetic words: "Do not be afraid; henceforth you will be catching men" (Luke 5:10 RSV). At this provocation both Peter and his companions laid their vows at Jesus' feet: "And when they brought their boats to the land, they left everything and followed him" (Luke 5:11 RSV). Christ had hooked his "fish." His next step would be to clean them and feed a multitude with their witness.

When Jesus says, "Follow me and I will make you," what does that mean? It means, first of all, that he himself is the object of faith. "Follow me" is not an idea to ponder, nor a philosophical principle to debate. Jesus knew who he was, where he came from, where he was going. He knew his objectives. He knew why he was alive. "Jesus knowing that the Father had given all things into his hands, and that he was come from God, and went to God; he riseth from supper, and laid aside his garments; and took a towel" (John 13:3-4). Great men can afford to stoop. These disciples were beholding the man Christ Jesus, chiefest among men yet servant of all.

The future that the disciples faced following Jesus would lead them into a life of servitude. But first there had to come to them an illumination. Peter would have the sensitivity to distinguish the fine lines of God etched on the face of Jesus. He would be able to see through the divine disguise and recognize Christ for whom the ages had sought and waited. He would knight the Savior with a name that is above every name. He would follow until he had received all the mind-stretching ideas, all the authentic emotions, and all the superlative plans that God reserves for his intimates.

It was a historic occasion when Peter recognized Jesus as the Christ at Caesarea Philippi. Yet in the very next breath Peter would display a blindness that appalled the Master and exposed his liability. There was much vacant territory in his mansoul where entrenched evil would resist the mind of Christ.

Peter resisted the *divine plan for salvation.* "From that time forth began Jesus to shew unto his disciples, how that he must go unto Jerusalem, and suffer many things . . . , and be killed, and be raised again the third day. Then Peter took him, and began to rebuke him, saying, Be it far from thee, Lord: this shall not be unto thee. But he turned, and said unto Peter, Get thee behind me, Satan: . . . for thou savourest [understand] not the things that be of God, but those that be of men" (Matt. 16:21–23). Peter could see no efficacy in the Cross and bade Christ bypass it. He wanted to sneak in the crown without a cross and arrive at sovereignty without suffering. His unaided human reason led him to believe that Jesus could do better in the political arena than in the prophetic office. He tended to think that the Kingdom would come with "swords loud clashing and roll of stirring drums" instead of that "deed of love and mercy" demonstrated at Calvary.

Peter resisted the *divine procedure of sanctification.* "After that he [Jesus] poureth water into a basin, and began to wash the disciples' feet. . . .Then cometh he to Simon Peter: and Peter saith unto him, Lord, dost thou wash my feet? . . . Thou shalt never wash my feet" (John 13:5, 6, 8). Peter knew what it was to love Jesus. But Peter had little understanding of Jesus. Peter was in a similar position to that of Peter Taylor Forsyth who once wrote, "I ceased becoming a lover of love and became an object of grace." That was Peter's situation that night in the Upper Room. "Thou shalt never wash my feet." Jesus answered, "If I wash thee not, thou hast no part with me." Then Peter called for a bath, "Lord, not my feet only, but also my hands and my head" (John 13:8, 9). Peter rejected the essential and sought the unnecessary.

Peter desired a quick means of sanctification.

But there is no substitute for obedient following. There is no shortage of people who want a cure-all experience that will give them immediate sanctity. But there are few who want to follow Jesus. Jesus never gave an alternative to obedience. So Peter asseverates, "Lord, why cannot I follow thee now? I will lay down my life for thy sake" (John 13:37).

Peter has been accused of being a braggart and a coward who belied these words. But I do not accept that assessment. Peter did follow Jesus. Or at least he attempted to do so. There was not a drop of cowardice in him. He was a man of raw courage. And when they came to arrest Jesus, Peter took out his sword to defend Him. He confronted armed men (either the temple police or Roman soldiery). It was not Peter's love that faltered. It was his faith. Jesus had said, "I have prayed for thee, that thy faith fail not." That faith maneuvered him into the High Priest's court. There Peter saw the spittle, the thorns and lacerations. He witnessed the Rose of Sharon being crushed beneath the beggar's heel; and disillusionment set in.

What was Peter's problem? He wanted to do something for Jesus. He wanted to wash Jesus' feet, protect his life, promote his safety, aid his ascendence to the throne. But Jesus said, "Where I am going you cannot follow me now, but . . . afterward" (John 13:36 RSV). Jesus had to go to the Cross alone. "There was no other good enough / To pay the price of sin." Peter could not contribute one iota to what Jesus did at the Cross. All that any of us can offer Jesus is the sin from which we need to be saved. That is hard for us to realize. Jesus had to do something for Peter first. He had to wash Peter's feet. He had to die for Peter. He had to rise for Peter. He had to invade the body of Peter with his own indwelling Presence. And the lesson Peter had to learn in following was the lesson of faith, which is our response to grace. It is always "afterward" that we follow Jesus.

Peter's denial of Christ was based not on cowardice but on frustration. He had the feeling that Christ himself was defeated, that even the promised Messiah of God could not get hold of the human situation. Who among us has not been tempted thus? To Peter's swelling words of self-assurance Jesus answered, "Verily, verily, I say unto thee, The cock shall not crow, till thou hast denied me thrice" (John 13:38).

Thus the same Lord who had directed the fish at sea to cooperate with him in *catching* Peter commands a rooster to assist him in *cleansing* Peter. The cock crows in yonder barnyard! It was God's signal to Peter of Christ's foreknowledge. "Satan hath desired to . . . sift you as wheat; but I have prayed for thee" (Luke 22:31). The reason that Jesus allowed the cock to crow *after* Peter denied him has long been enigmatic for me. Why not *before*? Why did he not warn Peter of this impending danger? The truth that I finally understand is

51

this: that rooster's cry indicated the morning was at hand. Peter had heard the welcome note across the Sea of Galilee. After many a weary night of fishing, the words had reviving power upon reaching his ears. "The night is far spent, the day is at hand!" There was hope even in the rebuke and bitter experience. It was in itself a prophecy that the old night of despondency and despair had been rolled back, and he was now embraced by a glorious new dawn, a fresh day of opportunity. There was no future in Peter's past, and no past in his future. The trumpet sounded a new beginning.

"What God gets he takes, what God takes he cleanses, what God cleanses he fills, what God fills he uses." That is Bible scholar F. B. Meyer's instructive epigram. And how that fits Peter—and us! God cleansed Peter with the dawn. "The eyes of your understanding being enlightened; that ye may know" (Eph. 1:18). The ministry of the Holy Spirit is associated more with illumination than with power.

So, Peter's first experience left him with a sense of iniquity or inequity with Jesus in that boat on the sea. Jesus was so pure and mighty, and Peter was so soiled and petty. Jesus used a fisherman's net to catch Peter. The second experience resulted in Peter's transgression. He had sworn and cursed and reverted to type. Jesus used a rooster's cry to bring cleansing to Peter.

Peter was brokenhearted over precisely the same three expressions of human depravity that

Moses prayed about in Exodus 34:7, "Keeping mercy for thousands, forgiving iniquity and transgression and sin." It is the same conviction that gripped brokenhearted David when he prayed, "Wash me thoroughly from mine iniquity, and cleanse me from my sin, for I acknowledge my transgressions" (Ps. 51:2–3). Iniquity! Transgression! Sin!

It is this same threefold revelation that comes to Peter. And his third confrontation is with his sin. He knew that he had missed the mark.

Peter must have been heavy with self-hate after the Crucifixion. He must have muttered to himself more than once, "You've blown it, Peter!" He was brokenhearted with despair. But despair is not a mark of intelligence. It is a spell of imbecility. It is to miss the summons of God in the high calling of Christ "which he wrought . . . when he raised him from the dead, and set him at his own right hand . . ., far above all principality, and power, and might, and dominion, and every name that is named, not only in this world, but also in that which is to come. . . . And hath raised us up together . . . in Christ Jesus" (Eph. 1:20–21; 2:6).

Peter had returned to his empty nets and empty nights. Contemplate the scene a week after the Crucifixion. The high priest had returned to his empty ritual and forsaken altars. Pilate had returned to his basin of water that had failed to wash away his guilt. And the fishermen had returned to their trade. It was evening. The lake was flecked with white as the stars danced upon it. The moon

53

sent down its beams like silver grappling hooks to move the tide and surge the sea. Seven followers of the Lord who could never forget the Unforgettable gathered around the little harbor in Capernaum. They pushed out to sea in their little boats with slanting sails, worn seats, and red rudders. At least they were comfortable with what they knew. They labored all night and caught nothing. As the sun began to crimson the Galilean mountains in the early morning, they rowed for port. They glimpsed the figure of a man standing on the shore calling to them. His voice trumpeted a heartening note: "Children, have ye any meat? They answered him, No. And he said unto them, Cast the net on the right side of the ship, and ye shall find. They cast therefore, and now they were not able to draw it for the multitude of fishes" (John 21:5–6). Old memories stirred. This was reminiscent of another night. Old chords of the heart began to vibrate once more. John turned to Peter: "It is the Lord!" That was enough. Peter, the extremist, tightened his fisher's tunic round his loins, leaped into the sea, swam across the hundred yards that separated him from the Lord, and put his dripping self at the feet of the Master. The others followed, bringing their boat loaded with 153 fishes.

Jesus had built a little fire on the shore, and breakfast awaited those weary disciples. One of the most poignant sentences in scripture shines exhilaratingly: "Jesus saith unto them, Come and dine. And none of the disciples durst ask him,

Who art thou? knowing that it was the Lord" (John 21:12).

After they had dined, Jesus turned to Peter with the most important question he ever put to the soul of man: "Simon Peter, son of Jonas, lovest thou me more than these?" (John 21:15). Three times it is repeated, and three times Peter responds in the affirmative. (Never mind the play on the use of the three Greek words for love.) Perhaps they were used to exorcise the triple guilt from that night of denial. But Jesus was not eliciting *repentance*. Peter had repented a thousand times. Nor was it *resolution*. Peter had resolved that he would follow Jesus to the death. It was *revival* that Jesus was after—the revival of love. "Lovest thou me more than these?" Jesus asked Peter. Then "feed my lambs. . . . Feed my sheep." Jesus was linking that love with mission. By a fisherman's net he *caught* Peter; by a crowing rooster he *cleansed* Peter; by a charcoal fire he *commissioned* Peter.

Jesus fed those discouraged disciples. They experienced the incomparable vitality of his seeking love and listened to his triumphant voice. He fed them with assurance. They were now to feed his sheep with that same assurance.

Frederick William Robertson of Brighton came upon days of discouragement. He wanted to resign his ministry. Christ came to him in that darkness after he too had rowed and toiled in ministry and had succeeded in catching nothing. He said to

55

Robertson, "You don't need to resign your commission; you need your commission 're-signed.'"

That is what happened to brokenhearted Peter. His unworthiness was swallowed up in Christ's new acceptance and assurance and ordination. He dropped the false estimate of himself. However low it had been, concerning his feelings, it was as high as heaven, concerning his calling.

DEATH—FRAUDULENT AND MOMENTARY

And he that was dead came forth, bound
hand and foot with graveclothes: . . . Jesus
saith unto them, Loose him, and let him
go.

John 11:44

The scene is Bethany. The occasion is the death of
Lazarus. Jesus has been summoned to this home.
As he enters the city he is met by Martha whose
greeting is, "Lord, if thou hadst been here, my
brother had not died" (John 11:21). "Jesus saith
unto her, Thy brother shall rise again" (11:23).
Martha replied, "I know that he shall rise again in
the resurrection at the last day" (11:24).

Martha had a problem—a dead brother. She
was looking backward, "If thou hadst been here."
And then she looked forward, "I know he shall
rise again in the resurrection at the last day." Or as
The Living Bible puts it, "Yes," Martha said,
"when everybody else does, on Resurrection
Day" (11:24 TLB).

But Martha's problem was not four days ago, nor at the last day. The problem was "in the now." This situation mirrors us. We look backward and say, "If only—if only I hadn't made that mistake," "If only I had chosen that job, made that investment, formed that friendship," "If only—if only." Or, if we do not fix our thinking on the past, we project to the future: "Someday," we surmise, "everything will be perfected concerning us, and we trust that God will take hold of the human situation." But between the "what might have been" of the past and the "what could be" of the future, we are suspended in the intolerable now.

All the while Jesus is standing in her midst saying, "Martha, right now I am the answer to your problem." I am! Christ always is on an I-am basis. This is a tremendous truth that we can hardly get our minds around because of its dimension. But let us try nevertheless. Jesus is God's absolute among all earth's relativisms. This truth enunciates the fact of God's existence and his eternality. Jesus Christ is a God who was and a God who will be. But the most prominent thing about Jesus is the fact that he is. "Thine is the Kingdom"! Not *was* or *will be* but *is*. Time goes and comes with us but not God. We are in time, but time is in God. This is the doctrine of the immanence of God. Not that God is in everything as though he were oozing out of the acorns, but everything is in him. "For in him we live, and

58

move, and have our being" (Acts 17:28). All days are in Jesus, including the last day.

I

Martha was intimidated by time. She was heartbroken over the death of her brother. Jesus asked her, "Where have ye laid him?" (John 11:34). In other words, "Where is the problem?" That is the question we must answer. Where is it we hurt? "Lord, it is in my heart," "It is in my thoughts," "It is in my body," "It is in my marriage," "It is in my relationship," "It is in my work," "It is in my church." Somewhere there remains a dead symbol of what once was a vibrant form, a vital feeling, or a vivid relationship.

Where is it? Come and see! They invited the One who revealed himself as the "I am" of God to reconnoiter their problem. Jesus is so identified with these who were sorrowful that he wept at the passing of Lazarus whom he loved. I do not think he was actually weeping for Lazarus because Lazarus would be called back from death in just a short while. Nor was he sorrowful for Mary and Martha, for they would soon be shouting with him the hallelujah chorus!

Jesus saw the obtuseness of these friends, and it hurt him. Their perspective was so imperfect. They loved the Master but did not have the eyes of their understanding enlightened to see death as he saw it. Jesus is so much one with us in our humanity that he can feel our infirmities and the limitations of our time-space relationships. But he so surpasses us that he can transcend this time-space circumference that encapsulates us. He can reach backward and forward and bring all time to a standstill. So there is both the *tear* and the *triumph*. He wept at this scene, but he also spoke a jubilant word into the milieu of trouble.

II

Having arrived at Lazarus' tomb Jesus makes a shocking request. He says, "Take away the stone!" Martha responds, "Lord, by this time he stinketh: for he hath been dead four days" (John 11:39).

Again we see, it was the passing of time and the barrier of distance that Martha could not negotiate. Neither can we. In all our moving in space and all our growing and decaying in time, Jesus remains the constant factor, the unchanging quantity. Someone has aptly called Jesus the "Everywhere who has come into the here and the All-Time who has come into the now." Christ is not shaken by the contingency of our time and space. He is only grieved because we are time's prisoners.

Lambert Dolphin, the scientist, has pointed out in one of his lectures that time is measured and recorded in some sense in our physical bodies but not in our spirits. That is the reason the early Christians could be shut up in prison, but their unfettered spirits leaped in freedom. In death that same human spirit simply leaves this earth and its time reference.

Until recently scientists have had no evidence with which to confirm or refute the Christian doctrine of immortality. Things are now changing, however. For example, the eminent psychiatrist Dr. Elisabeth Kübler-Ross has talked to hundreds of people who have undergone a "death experience" and have been resuscitated. They all report an observed departure of spirit from body. Dr. Kübler-Ross considers this scientific proof.

On December 20, 1943, Dr. George G. Richey, Jr., was pronounced dead by an army physician and nurse at Camp Barkley, Texas. In the book *The Vestibule* by Jesse Weiss, Dr. Richey reports leaving his body and seeing a figure on the table with slack jaw, gray skin; and to his great astonishment he recognized himself. He stepped into the corridor where an orderly passed right through him. There followed a series of attempts to get to Richmond, Virginia, where he was to enter medical school. He was frustrated because he could not communicate with the faculty counselor, nor make himself known to anyone. In desperation he went back to the hospital to find and reenter his own body. All this happened in a matter of moments.

I do not wish to comment on the authenticity of such an experience. Granted, we are dealing in extraterrestrial material that defies our limited experience. But it points us to a transcendent truth hinted at in scripture. Stephen, for example, was time-transported into the future and saw Jesus standing at the right hand of the Father. Elsewhere in scripture Jesus is pictured standing at the time of the Resurrection. Though this event has not yet occurred for us, it seems that Stephen entered the "eternal now" where Jesus is the fixed point. If indeed Jesus is the "Lamb slain from the foundation of the world" (Rev. 13:8), then with God everything has already happened. C. S. Lewis said, "If one pictures time as a straight line along which we have to travel, then we must picture God as the whole page on which that line is drawn." How provocative then is Bishop Leslie Newbigin when he declares, "To know God, the living God, means to live in the constant expectancy of what is new, yet in the constant certainty that nothing which happens can contradict the reality of what has been revealed."

Would it not be proper for us to conclude then that all Christians will arrive in heaven at the same moment; that when death occurs, we may turn to see Stephen, Paul, Wesley, and all our Christian friends and family arriving at the same time? The scripture says, "In a moment, in the twinkling of an eye, at the last trump: . . . we shall be changed" (I Cor. 15:52).

Last times, end times, and *the last day* are all relative terms. A great many people are attempting to ascertain where we are in time relative to the last day. Some say we are there now; and so we are. The last days commenced on the day of Christ's ascension. The question is, Are we in the last moments of the last days? The answer is, we do not know. But we do know that the end of the age is upon us. The Christian has already "tasted the good word of God, and powers of the world to come" (Heb. 6:5). In Christ, time loses its deceiving hold upon our minds, and we are linked with eternity. "To be absent from the body, and present with the Lord" means all relativism will be gone forever. We will be with Jesus who is in the throne room of eternity.

III

In a recent book called *Appointment with Death*, Alvin Rogness speaks of death's triumph over the earthly life of the Christian as fraudulent and momentary. In reality it is the victory of Christ's life over death that is forever. One saint who had lost her husband to death was reading over the passage II Peter 3:8, "But, beloved, be not ignorant of this one thing, that one day is with the Lord as a thousand years, and a thousand years as one day." The widow asked an electronics expert to compute the ratio of a lifespan to eternity. And the answer was given. The average human lifespan is one hour and fifteen minutes. A great flood of joy was released in her spirit, and she exclaimed, "Hallelujah, my husband always was an impatient man. I suppose he's not anxious anymore since he knows that he has only fifteen minutes to wait, and I'll be there with him." In reality it won't

63

THOSE HE CAME TO SAVE

even be fifteen minutes, but the relativity of time must always be taken into account when we stand at the biers of our loved ones. As we come nearer to Christ, we come nearer to all those who are in him. This is the meaning of the communion of saints. The saints cannot bring us to Jesus, but Jesus can bring us to the saints. If we love and trust him, all things will come to us as he orders them, even death.

Lazarus was allowed to die in order to fulfill a higher purpose. It was not in death that God was glorified; it was in resurrection. Resurrection does not carry Jesus; he carries the Resurrection. We are not death's victims but death's victors because we believe that Jesus' life is triumphant. His deathless life is in each Christian. He did not come to offer some academic speculation about death. He came to shout a clear defiance in the face of death. He did not talk about death, he talked to death. Death did not convert him, he converted death. He repudiated its hold on the human race. He did more; he shattered it! He throttled it! He forever defeated it! He came forth from a stranger's grave to show the breast where a Roman spear had made forever visible a heart that loved us enough to die for us and that lives on to love us eternally.

IV

"I am! Do you believe it? Show me your problem. Set it in the light of who I am," says Jesus.

There is a striking and superlative statement about Jesus Christ in Revelation 19:16, "And he hath on his vesture and on his thigh a name written, KING OF KINGS AND LORD OF LORDS." That is, he lords it over everything that lords it over us, including death. "Knowing that Christ being raised from the dead dieth no more; death hath no more dominion over him" (Rom. 6:9).

Expose the problem: "Then they took away the stone" (John 11:41). There was nothing between the problem and Jesus Christ, the Mediator between God and man. There is nothing to prevent the Son of God from dealing with that human dilemma, for it is opened before him. Sometimes in our pride we do not really want to confess our plight. We have some impressive epitaph on our tombstone and do not wish for any to see the corruption that lies beneath the surface. It is so unsavory.

But Jesus is not at all shocked. He knows what is behind our facades. He understands us perfectly and loves us preeminently. So we need never fear sharing our burdens, exposing our problems, confessing our sins to the Son of God. "Never expect Christ to cover with his blood that which you will not uncover," spoke the late Duncan Campbell.

With the whole corruptible matter opened to him, Jesus speaks into that deadness, into the context of their sorrow and despair, "Lazarus, come forth!" The scripture tells us that he "cried with a loud voice" (John 11:43). Apart from that loud cry on the Cross, there is only one other occasion of Christ's raising his voice in anything like a shout. That is found in I Thessalonians 4:16, "For the Lord himself shall descend from heaven with a shout, . . . and the dead in Christ shall rise first." When Jesus raised the widow's son of Nain, and Jairus' daughter, he spoke in soft tones. But when he raised Lazarus, and subsequently when he raises all the righteous dead in Christ at the last day, he shouts. Rufus Moseley used to say that it only proves that the longer one is dead, the louder Jesus has to shout.

V

Lazarus comes forth. But he is "bound hand and foot with graveclothes" (John 11:44). So Jesus speaks once again: "Loose him, and let him go." Jesus resurrects those who are "dead in sins" so that he might restore to them the true content of their humanity: life! "I am the resurrection, and the life," he said to Martha (John 11:25). "I am the resurrection to those who are dead and the life to those who are living" is doubtless the intended meaning.

Jesus knew full well it would be possible for us to be called out of the grave of spiritual death and still be bound by wrappings from the old life. So half the New Testament is written to Christians, admonishing them to live the life that has been provided. We are reminded that life is predicated in victory, that freedom is a part of our inheritance. We are offered a present power for a thoroughgoing triumph. There is flushed into the bloodstream of every believer a life that makes us, in all things, "more than conquerors."

Christ offers release from the old encumbrances of life. He affords us a freedom from fear of the future as well as freedom from the memory of the past. He strikes the bonds that would tether us to the stake of human despair. He sweeps from our souls the anxiety that chokes life. And he gives us "a garment of praise for the spirit of heaviness."

The difference between Lazarus and Jesus is that Jesus left his graveclothes behind him as he emerged from that tomb on Easter morning. Lazarus came out bound. These graveclothes represent the old way of thinking: proclivities of the past that bind us to ineffective living. Lazarus had his mouth bound. He could not freely communicate the new life that was his. His feet were bound. He could not follow the Lord freely. His hands were bound. He could not "lift up holy hands without wrath and doubting," in order to receive blessings in answer to prayer.

The good news to those brokenhearted over their deadness is that "the law of the spirit of life in Christ Jesus" sets us free from "the law of sin and death." The Christian is not world denying. He is life affirming. When the risen life of Christ dominates, death lays down its arms and retreats from the battlefield of mansoul.

GOOD NEWS
TO THE BOUND

He hath sent me . . . to preach deliverance
to the captives.
Luke 4:18

LOOSED FROM LEGION

Malcolm Muggeridge has described our age as
"nihilistic in purpose, ethically and spiritually
vacuous and Gadarene in its direction." *Gadarene
direction* turns us immediately to Luke 8. Jesus
came to the shores of Gadara near Galilee. He saw
helpless citizens standing by, gazing listlessly at a
lunatic in a graveyard. This demented man was
destroying himself and creating furtive restive-
ness in the community. What a picture of the
insanity that causes a society to accept national
and international anarchy as the norm.

As Jesus approached, the man bound by a legion of demons screamed with agonizing dissent:
"What have I to do with thee, Jesus, thou Son of

God most high? I beseech thee, torment me not. (For he had commanded the unclean spirit to come out of the man. For oftentimes it had caught him; and he was kept bound with chains and in fetters; and he brake the bands, and was driven of the devil into the wilderness)" (Luke 8:28–29).

This bizarre picture thrusts into prominent profile our modern human dilemma. We too are shadowed by the sinister symbols of a graveyard. We cut and lash our bodies with frustrating emotions. We assault and exploit our natural resources. Our planet is fast becoming an ugly revolving morgue of pollution and decay. We ourselves are bound in the chains of self-defeating habits and systems.

But worst of all, when the only true and healthy Man of history comes to offer his help we resist him and cry, "What have we to do with thee, Jesus?" Bishop Stephen Neill of south India alluded to this endemic element of perversion in man when he wrote:

I have never been able to understand why, in contemporary history-writing, the Christian is never permitted to be right. Everyone else is allowed to be intolerant, but not he. Marxism is the most intolerant creed of history, but the Marxist is regarded as more than respectable. . . . Marxists, Muslims, modern Vedantists, are all active propagandists, and make no secret of their desire to convert others to their views. To this no objection seems to be raised. But let a Christian attempt to convert anyone else to his faith and he is immediately accused of western arrogance

69

and of attempting to impose on others an alien—and purely western faith.

Is this not saying, "What have [we] to do with thee, Jesus, thou Son of God most high?" (Luke 8:28).

Our name, too, is legion. For we are disordered in our minds. Thomas Boston scores our times in that old Scottish classic *The Fourfold State:*

> The natural man's affections are wretchedly misplaced: he is a spiritual monster. His heart is, where his feet should be, fixed on the earth; his heels are lifted up against heaven, which his heart should be set on (Acts 9:5). His face is towards hell, his back towards heaven, and therefore God calls him to turn. He loves what he should hate, and hates what he should love; joys in what he ought to mourn for, and mourns for what he should rejoice in; glorieth in his shame, and is ashamed for his glory; abhors what he should desire, and desires what he should abhor (Proverbs 2:13–15).

That is an apt description of a generation that is, as Francis Shaeffer puts it, "escaping from reason." And in typical trenchant observation, the shrewd and startling G. K. Chesterton has said clearly, "When we turn from the true God, we don't turn to nothing, we turn to everything." So the mind of man is dominated by legion, a complexity of conflicting desires and purposes. Legion is our name, all right. "Leave me alone!" is our disposition toward the only saving Person of history. But Jesus Christ is not put off by our recalcitrance. When he has finished, order has come to a fragmented mind. This man is found "sitting at the feet of Jesus, clothed, and in his right mind" (Luke 8:35). That mighty liberation results in:

Deliverance from Vanity

Was the Gadarene in this plight because his imagination had become vain? Civilization is led to the brink by those whose imaginations have become darkened (see Rom. 1:21). Further, in the Ephesian Letter we are told of those Gentiles who "walk, in the vanity of their mind" (4:17). Moreover, the decadent society described in Ephesus came about by men "fulfilling the desires of the flesh and of the mind." The world at large is captive to lustful and vain thinking. It would at first appear that lust belongs to a category different from that of the mind. But this is the divine diagnosis. Ask the average university student what he believes and he will tell you that he believes what his mind tells him to believe. His mind is the ultimate datum. His mind is his god. And his god is Legion.

James propounds the question, "From whence come wars and fightings among you?" Then he proposes the answer, "Come they not hence, even of your lusts that war in your members?" (James 4:1). Man cannot find sustained and viable solutions to his problems because his mind is under the enthrallment of lust. This lust has a tremendous power that pulls him under bondage: "drawn away of his own lust, and enticed" (1:14).

71

Jesus comes to our Gadarene society to set the mind at liberty. The mind is made to think God's thoughts. "For I know the thoughts that I think toward you, saith the Lord, thoughts of peace, and not of evil, to bring you to an expected end" (Jer. 29:11). The mind is made for Christ just as the lungs are made for air and the eyes for light. The mind was never given to make men brilliant any more than the law was given to make the Jews just. The law was there to be fulfilled in Christ, and the mind is there for the same reason. "Let this mind be in you, which was also in Christ Jesus" (Phil. 2:5). We have the same eyes at noon that we have at midnight, but we cannot see as well at midnight because light is not reflected in our eyes. Light comes from an external revelation that is refracted and reflected through our eyes.

We walk in the vanity of our minds when we ignore the revelation of God and attempt to assess life without reference to the Word of God. When we set up our minds as the ultimate authority for what is right and what is wrong, for what is good and what is bad, for what is God and what is not God, that is sheer vanity. It is not what we think about God that is primarily important, it is what we discover to be God's thoughts about us. Our thoughts are but poor reflections of his thoughts. We are shut up to only two alternatives; speculative philosophy or divine revelation. Those who take the way of human philosophy are described in Romans, "They . . . became vain in their imaginations, and their foolish heart was darkened.

Professing themselves to be wise, they became fools" (1:21–22). Bible scholar R. A. Torrey, commenting on this verse, paraphrased it, "Professing themselves to be wise, they became 'foolosophers.'" Any man who puts his feeble mind up against the all-knowingness of God is a fool—a double-distilled, triple-extracted, stamped-on-the-cork, blown-on-the-bottle, fourteen karat, copper-lined fool!

Professors will stagger the minds of the young with the brilliance of their negations, but in the light of eternity it is totally irrelevant! God's view is important and relevant.

The opposite of "walking in the vanity of the mind" is "walking in love." For the Christian the ultimate dictum is not the mind but the love of God. "Walk not as other Gentiles walk, in the vanity of their minds. . . . Be ye . . . followers of God, as dear children; and walk in love" (Eph. 4:17, 5:1–2).

When we ask for Christ to leave us alone, it is not our reason but our irrationality. It is our jabbering foolishness, not our higher wisdom; it is our hostility, not our hope.

Deliverance from Insanity

"What have I to do with thee, Jesus, thou Son of God most high?" (Luke 8:28). The answer is, "Much, if we want to maintain our sanity." He is the One who confronts us as "the most high God" in his omniscience. He is God's absolute among

73

all the relativisms of life. Yet our society has adopted relativism as its very life-style. Literature, drama, politics, ethics, science—these disciplines refuse to bow to the claims of his absolute lordship. But bow they must if there is to be an integrated center to gather up our chaos and conserve our universe. A reviewer in the *New York Times* said of a play on Broadway: "The constant pre-occupation of the characters [of this play] with the petty and frivolous pursuits makes one feel that outright insanity would be an intellectual promotion for them."

Lack of moral authority leads to insanity. When we don't know where the goal posts are, the game of life is nonsense. This generation has to a large extent thrown away the rules but wants to get on with the game. They ask, "What is morality?" And we answer, "Right conduct!" But right according to what? According to whom? It is right according to the truth about life, the truth about man, the truth about God, the truth about the world. In a court of law, truth is correspondence to fact; but in religion, truth is correspondence to God. If we have no absolute revelation of God in Jesus Christ, then we have no categories. If we have no categories, then there is no right and wrong; there is only right and left.

With such a disposition we can very readily set up our own mind to be the absolute arbiter of all things. This will mean that others are to the right or left according to our standard of thinking. It follows, then, that all moral and ethical decisions will be considered relative. Relativism is the watchword of a generation that loves darkness more than light. The condition of that dark historical period when the Judges ruled over Israel exists today. Recurrent throughout the book and closing with the final chapter is the sad commentary that "in those days there was no king in Israel: every man did that which was right in his own eyes" (21:25). Not that which was wrong, mind you. But that which was "right in his own eyes." That's relativism that leads to anarchy. Because we have no absolutes, we have no categories—beyond technological and pragmatic ones. And because there are no categories, there is no meaning left in our words.

Someone has taken no less an authority than the dictionary to show us how we can thus be led imperceptibly away from the truth. Take the dictionary and try it. The word *black* means "dark." Trace the word *dark*. It means "obscure." *Obscure* can be defined as "dim," and *dim* means "pale." *Pale* then is rendered as "white." The difference in each case is so subtle that we are not aware of being moved to the position that *black* means "white."

The very word *relativism* implies that there is an absolute, else to what is an idea or matter relative? Time, for example, is relative, and we would have confusion if everyone kept his own brand. But there is a standard of absolute time. We call it Greenwich time. We must have this to serve as a point of reference. Then with a knowledge of the longitude where we are situated, we can proceed on schedule around the world without confusion. So with our minds when they are calibrated by the Word of God. Jesus is God's categorical imperative, his celestial sphere of order approaching our hemisphere of disorder, his omniscience approaching our finite science.

Deliverance from Futility

Someone has defined *cancer* as a "cell that didn't believe it mattered." Could this have been the case of the Gadarene? Was his wild behavior a protest against a system that ground him to the dust and made him believe he was a zero with the cipher rubbed out? Did he consider himself the hapless and hopeless victim of outside forces that bent his destiny around some pole of despair? Or had some mystery religion got to him? Perhaps he had received some maya that exposed him to the demonic, and what he thought would be bliss turned out to be blight. Had some philosophy of promised tranquil unity brought rather the yowl of frantic demonism? Or was his mental aberration his refuge from moral failure to face what life demanded of him? Had no one told him that he was dear to God, planned for by a benevolent will? Was there no bright hope such as burned in the heart of Simeon for the consolation of Israel? Was there no loving expectation that pulled him forward and integrated him around a joyful acceptance of himself?

What was the world view that dominated his thinking? What theological concepts or lack of them forged his mind into a convoluted horror house of irrationality?

Was he a casualty of an orthodox religion that reproached instead of revived, killed joy rather than gave life, set up straw men instead of seeing the unrecognized man? Was he the one who believed that God was an "austere man, taking up where he had not laid down and reaping where he had not sown"?

Sometimes this false and fatal thinking is fortified by theology. There is the exaggerated and apocryphal story of the Presbyterian who fell down the stairs and landed somewhat ingloriously in the cellar. He rose to his feet, slowly brushed off his clothes, and said, "I'm glad that's over!"

We must be sure we read the heart of God aright through the scriptures. "God hath not appointed us to wrath, but to obtain salvation by our Lord Jesus Christ" (I Thess. 5:9).

Man's unhinged logic leads to despair and shuts out the kingdom of God. Aldous Huxley's fallen reason led him to say, "There is no such thing as forgiveness." George Bernard Shaw, under the same mental tent said, "Forgiveness is a beggar's refuge; we must pay our debts." To all this, James S. Stewart made reply, "Thanks for the information, but it is not your hidebound logic; it is heaven's grace that reigns!"

To thousands of others hooked on humanistic

categories that bind them to futility, frustration, and fear Jesus advances to the rescue. As a Gadara citizenry sits passively, gazing at the lunatic policies of men and nations, in utter helplessness, Jesus autocratically forces our attention. Our very survival depends upon the mind of man being brought again into captivity to the obedience of Christ's Lordship.

LOOSED FROM LITTLENESS

In the realm of the spirit, men are bound by littleness. Jesus taught us that God is magnanimous.
He is plentiful in mercy and gives on a grand scale.
When he wants space, he pushes back its bound-
aries to infinity. When he wants beauty, he car-
pets the ranging hills and meadows with daisies
and buttercups. When he forgives, he forgives
literally all our iniquities; and when he pardons,
he does so abundantly. He lives to make all
generosity accrue to us. "And God is able to make
all grace abound toward you; that ye, always having all sufficiency in all things, may abound to
every good work" (II Cor. 9:8).

Despite this fact, we are held in the grip of a
poverty complex. We can't think of enough health

to last our lifetime; so we are always getting ready to be sick. We can't conceive of God's having enough resources; so we become selfish and petty. We can't imagine God's being so ingenious as to make originals of us; so we attempt to imitate others. The quickest way to be a nobody is to be like everybody.

Dr. Clovis Chappell tells how as a student he boarded a train traveling from Boston to New York. At New Haven a friend joined him. He was a Yale student also, heading for New York. When they were seated, young Chappell spotted his companion's railway ticket protruding from his pocket and mischievously slipped it out. A few minutes later the student missed the ticket and told Clovis of his loss. The practical joke continued as Clovis feigned searching for it. At last the student admitted it was hopelessly lost and that he had no money for his fare. Clovis answered that he too was penniless but offered a suggestion. He told the friend to get under the seat as best he could, and he would spread his overcoat over him so the conductor would not see him. The boy reluctantly consented. But he had not been long in this humiliating and uncomfortable position when the conductor came by. Clovis gave him the two tickets, his own and the one he had slipped from his friend's pocket. "Where is the other passenger?" the conductor asked. "He is under the seat," Clovis answered. "He just prefers to ride that way."

The story is undoubtedly apocryphal, but it

does portray the posture of too many folks who are journeying through life. They don't feel that they are worthy to be accepted among God's beloved. They travel furtively and constrictively. The facts about God and life and human destiny have been hidden from them.

We entertain little thoughts toward other people. We cannot entertain big thoughts about God and little thoughts toward our fellows. That would be like trying to square a circle. Jesus told a dramatic story about this in the parable of the unwise steward. This man had accumulated a huge debt that he could not possibly liquidate. In utter desperation he went to his creditor and said,

> Lord, have patience with me, and I will pay thee all. Then the lord of that servant was moved with compassion, and loosed him, and forgave him the debt. But the same servant went out, and found one of his fellow servants [who owed him a pittance in comparison] . . . and took him by the throat, saying, Pay me that thou owest. . . . And [he] besought him, saying, Have patience with me. . . . And he would not; but went and cast him into prison, till he should pay the debt. . . . And his lord was wroth, and delivered him to the tormentors. . . . So likewise shall my heavenly Father do also unto you, if ye from your hearts forgive not every one his brother their trespasses. (Matt. 18:26–35)

There is simply no room in the heavenly order for any man, regardless of affiliation, who has allowed hatred, resentment, malice, jealousy, or scorn to possess his heart. He must be big toward his fellowman. A dwarf "shall not come nigh to offer the bread of his God" (Lev. 21:20). God is set against littleness. He wants us free from the spiritual captivity that shrinks our soul and perverts our perspective.

To the Corinthian church that was beleaguered with the problems of pettiness, Paul wrote a word that struck at the root of their troubles: "Be ye also enlarged" (II Cor. 6:13). No more graphic picture of this could have been recorded than the story of Zacchaeus in Luke 19. It portrays the action of God moving to enlarge a soul until in deep-wrought deliverance he reaches the stature of sheer magnanimity.

I

Luke tells us that Zacchaeus, the tax-collector "sought to see Jesus who he was; and could not for the press, because he was little of stature" (19:3). Zacchaeus had to be given a new altitude, a new elevation. That speaks to us of the human dilemma. Something has gone wrong with our stature. We have become a generation of shrunken sophisticates. We are scientifically sharp but spiritually shabby. Intolerance, greed, self-aggrandizement, vitiate the achievements that could expand our self-consciousness and secure our happiness.

Swept by the currents of men, we are manipulated by those who control the world's media. We are simply too small of stature to see over the mass. We are slaves to the domination of the ideas of men and captives to our culture. We have a limited horizon. It is impossible for us to elevate ourselves above our horizon of doubt, fear, and death. Interposed between us and ultimate contentment in life is the Titanic fact of the Fall.

This Fall stands at the fountainhead of our history. We are dwarfed and stunted not because God created us this way. This condition is the result of forfeiting our right to reign in life by one Jesus Christ. We have imbibed the Adamic lie that makes us think we can be the ruler of our own kingdom, the source of our own satisfaction, the origin of our own image, and the cause of our own effect. We are like the woman who was asked, "Which is more important, the sun or the moon?" She replied, "Why, the moon, of course! It shines at night when we need it. The sun shines in the day when it is light anyway."

But we are deceived. The historical lie is lodged at the root of history. The pride of man leads him to believe that he can search for the good and the true and come up with viable solutions to his human dilemma. That is the basis for so many of our educational presuppositions—that by searching we can find truth. Jesus did not say blankly, "Ye shall know the truth, and the truth shall make you free." What Jesus did say was, "If ye continue in my word, . . . ye shall know the truth, and the truth shall make you free" (John 8:31–32). It is the entrance of his word that gives light. Light is not something *for* which we search. It is something *by* which we search. According to Colossians, Jesus Christ is the light with which we must begin. He is the light on God, on creation, on government, on the nature of the church, on the mystery of eternity, on the assessment of true greatness, and on the reality of fulfillment. It is by his light that we see light (see Ps. 36:9).

The light of Christ lifts us as the sun lifts the plant life out of the ground. We cannot enjoy the expanding glories of life without this elevation of our spirits by the divine Spirit. The very capacity God has given us to appreciate life has been darkened and depraved by the Fall. The Ephesian writer describes such a life as one that drifts along on the stream of "this world's ideas of living" (see 2:2 Phillips). Animated corpses! Men circulate in society. They are alive to beauty, to the glow and wonder of a sunset, to the dancing laughter on a child's face, to the exquisite joy of home and family; they are alive to the physical pleasures that attend them day by day. But they are dead to the reality and purpose of it all!

You have met folks like that. They live in another world. They belong to another power. They are under another rule. This is what constitutes lostness. Lostness is not necessarily badness. It is awayness. The lamb was lost because it was away from the fold. The branch was lost because it was not in union with the vine. When Jesus said, "I have come . . . that you might have life" (John 10:10 TEV), he was not standing in a graveyard. He was addressing himself to those who join the laughing crowds, circulate in society, occupy seats of authority in human affairs. He was speaking to men who had laid hold upon a tantalizing nothingness that they thought was life but which was destitute of any compensating joys.

In the economy of truth there are only two men. There is the first Adam who was made a living soul and the last Adam who was made a quickening spirit (see I Cor. 15:46). Many live in the realm of the soul. When we live in the soul realm (mind, will, emotions) without reference to the spirit of Christ in us, we live only on an animal level. The light of the soul is the human spirit. Without the quickening of the human spirit by the divine Spirit the soul gets its motivation from its environment and is constantly elated or depressed by carnal stimuli.

A casual churchgoer emerged from a Christmas program after hearing a boys' choir perform. Oozing with sentiment, she remarked to the pastor, "Oh, how inspiring! That singing made chills go up and down my spine." The pastor replied, "The same effect could be produced by scraping my fingernails across a chalkboard!"

If one is after spine-tingling emotional jags, there is much afforded one in the modern church. But if one wishes to rub up against the grace of a forgiving God and be lifted to some windswept height where he can breathe pure air and see the light of hope again, then the spirit of man must be made alive and raised up together with Christ, to be seated with him in the heavenly places (see Eph. 2:5–6).

II

Zacchaeus climbed a tree. Here is the answer to our littleness. It is almost paradoxical, for climbing a tree is returning to childhood. To become a Christian is to become child*like* but not child*ish*. To be childlike is to get down off the high horse of our arrogant self-sufficiency. Jesus could do no mighty works in Nazareth because of their unbelief. He ran astride a haughty, puffed-up human ego. It was the proud thought that no man could be a success unless he came from the right family, attended the right schools, quoted the right authorities, and was seen in the right company. But fishermen and shepherds were humbled to the dust. The light of heaven pierced the despair of their souls. A new creative love broke upon the dull monotony of their defeat and drudgery.

To become a child again is to gain a new perspective from which the issues of life become clearer to us. It is a recognition of the disproportion of what we are and what God is. It is an acknowledgment of our weakness and sin. It means putting off worldly wisdom, pride, and superiority. We stand before the incalculable mystery of the incarnation of the Son of God. He who was so high became so low, to lift us to the heights. We become childlike enough to be reborn in old age.

Zacchaeus had a serious handicap. Morally he was dishonest. He was a publican and followed no principle but expediency. He was socially stigmatized. He was rich, and while it is not a sin to be rich, it is dangerous. For hardly will a rich man enter the kingdom of God. It is a matter of displaced trust. He was physically stunted. But all these impediments were overcome when he climbed the tree. He broke from the herd. It may be undignified to climb a tree, but it is the first step away from the artificialities of a sophisticated society that demands conformity. Even today's nonconformists can tolerate anything but nonconformity to their nonconformity. He was beginning to become a person. Jesus, picking him out of the crowd, called him by his name. Conversion is the beginning of being a person again. Outside of Christ we have lost our true identity. We are only a flaw in the void.

The spirit of a child sees with the eyes of faith. That spirit towers over the horizons of human limitations and sees the new creation of God hidden behind the ugly shape of the mass mind.

III

The drama of salvation unfolds in a mighty transformation. Zacchaeus, head of the tax-gatherers, was a wealthy man living in Jericho, the city of the palms, a veritable Eden. Here Mark Antony had become a recluse, and Herod the Great had died. In the air lingered the perfume of roses and balsam. Here publicans and courtiers rubbed shoulders with the traders moving along the great caravan route from the north and east. Zacchaeus had money and position, power and riches. We would think he could have risen to satisfaction and have gained proper stature. But a disturbing thing happened. A Man was moving in his midst, One who cared for neither wealth nor position. In fact, he was calling men to renounce both and to follow him. That new kind of life bumped like a thud against all Zacchaeus had built up as the ends of life.

When Zacchaeus looked upon Jesus, he saw stature that he had never gained. He saw a true son of Abraham, the true content of humanity. He saw the Erect among the fallen, the Pure among the defiled, the Great among the glamorous, the Man of the Ages among the men of the hour, the Living among the dead. And what he saw, shot a beam of light in his soul that quickened him.

Everything we see in Jesus by way of valor and virtue, by way of nobility and stature, God has in mind for us. Jesus awakened a dormant desire in Zacchaeus, creating a new hunger. Jesus said, "When you pray, whatsoever you desire, believe and you will receive it." The big thing is desire. We talk in flowing praise of Jesus Christ. But, paradoxically, when we see him, he usually has to say, "Don't be afraid." There is something frightening and awesome about Jesus. I am not sure I always want it. I see in him a reckless abandon to the will of God. I see a man who is not essentially a hedonistic, self-indulgent type. I see, rather, a purposeful, work-oriented, self-giving type, and I am not sure I want to live that way. If I were more honest, I might not sing "My desire is to be like Jesus." I would more honestly sing "My desire is to make him like me." But the Holy Spirit convicts me and makes me know that the kingdom of God is not fulfilled in terms of me but of him. Jesus is God's fulfillment of God's idea about man.

The story of Zacchaeus is set in the framework of this wonderful asseveration, "The Son of man is come to seek and to save that which was lost" (Luke 19:10). We use the word *lost* in terms of something final, desperate, and inexorable. And that is quite so apart from the gospel. But when Jesus uses the word, he uses it literally. When a man is lost, he doesn't know where he is, and that is a very different sense from just wandering. The very use of the word *lost* to describe the human race suggests hope, not despair, because only something that belongs somewhere can be lost. We go into the deep woods and see animals scurrying through the bushes. We do not say they are lost. But if a child is in those woods, search parties are organized. It is not where the child belongs.

Man as a fallen creature should not be given a gloomy diagnosis. A fallen creature can rise again, whereas if man were created as an evil-natured being, the situation would be hopeless.

It is futile to attempt to improve our old life. We

need to find our life by losing it in the will of God. We must be reoriented to the kingdom of God, otherwise all our expectations will go unrewarded. We are but multiplying our lostness and nothingness. William Newell said he once prayed, "Lord, make me nothing!" God answered, "You are nothing, accept it by faith." Sometimes a bit of humor parries the pride of our sophistication.

It is told that the early Methodist converts were social outcasts. During the early days of Wesley's outdoor evangelism, his converts were taken from the lowest social strata. Some wag suggested that the Methodists took them out of the gutter; the Baptists washed them in the waters of baptism; the Presbyterians educated them; the Episcopalians introduced them to the right people; whereupon the Methodists had to get them out of the gutter again!

It is our trying to be, apart from vital union with Jesus Christ, that shrinks life back down to the gutter level. But when I see him, I rise to a new level of expectancy. My true self emerges.

Look at the saints. They never knew themselves until they saw in Jesus a reflection of their true identity. Lost in the wonder of Christ, they came into their own.

This is the basis of all true freedom. Most of us are aware that Columbus discovered America in 1492; yet there was no serious attempt at colonization until 1620. We would do well to look at this span of history. The French were in Canada; the

Spaniards were in Florida. If either of these powers had developed the new world, our form of government would have been drastically different—monarchical rather than democratic.

The reason for this rather stagnant interim of history is quite apparent. It was the evangelical revival on the Continent that gave men a new concept of God, man, and human destiny. They began to read the Bible and find out who they were. They were sacred because the royal blood of God had been poured out for them. Their sanctity was the basis of their dignity. They dropped their inhibitions and small thoughts. Realizing they were not born to wear the chains of tyranny, they broke into a new world. They were born free. Into the hearts of a people who had known nothing but beggarly and niggardly ways, a new hope emerged, and a new dimension of life came.

They were the heirs of those who, like Zacchaeus, looked into the face of Jesus Christ and were brought out of the dark prisons of their fallen images. They came forth with the New Testament in their hands. Exiles and refugees marched across Europe with the seeds of the Reformation in their hearts. They were people of God, not slaves of the state. They were born for big things. They had capacity to become sons of God. Life was not intended as a predatory struggle for bread but for eternal comradeship with Christ. No dwarfish, stunted ideas dominated them. They held democracy in their brains. The whole concept of freedom, equality, and fraternity was born in their unshackled minds. They climbed into their worm-eaten ships, not to build another empire, but to establish an orderly process of government in which the right of private judgment, free conscience, free press, free pulpit, and the open Bible could take root and flourish.

Christ is the source of our freedom. Zacchaeus fell under Christ's beneficent countenance and became Christ's freeman. A shepherd boy found His mercy seat and rose to a throne; an obscure Jewish girl caught the intent of the divine heart and became queen of Medo-Persia. A baby boy abandoned on the Nile River was lured out by the providence of this loving Lord and became a prince in Egypt and the Lincoln of the Old Testament. Ishmael, smeared by ignominy, came under the compassionate gaze of this gracious God and was made the sovereign of the desert, and his seed now presides over half the earth's known oil supply. Ignorant and unlearned fishermen were stimulated by this liberating Christ and became ambassadors of a Kingdom that knows no end. He unlooses the bound, then binds us to himself that we may experience life's liberating secret.

LOOSED FROM LIMITATIONS

Of all the New Testament writers, it is Luke who seems to pick up the distress signals of humanity. The gospel is "good tidings of great joy, which shall be to all people" (Luke 2:10). He makes the book of Acts show how evangelism is written large in global dimension. He has Peter and John moving outside the temple in Jerusalem and gives us a portrait of the effect of this good news for those who are bound by limitations.

A crippled man was healed as Peter and John spoke the word of faith, "In the name of Jesus Christ of Nazareth rise up and walk" (Acts 3:6). This paralytic had sat for years on end at the beautiful gate of the temple. The Bible tells us he was lame from birth. Something was wrong from the

93

beginning. And there he sits, with a liability that separates him from all his hopes and aspirations. His childhood stunted, his manhood frustrated, his life a caricature—a travesty of what life was meant to be. Bound to misery, bound to helplessness, bound to ineffectiveness, but the sad thing is this: he had ceased to expect anything better. The will to walk and run had left him. He had become content with the life of a beggar.

There is no one so infirm as the man who has lost the will to be, who lives without the sense of the high calling of God, whose motto is forward but not upward, whose goal is success but not wholeness, who has ambition but no aspiration, whose life is lived without the sense of the overarching sky of God's loving plan.

This beggar was content with alms when all the illimitable resources of life were being poured out all around him. He was living in the days of Pentecost and the effusion of power, but he was begging for a living at the very gates of life.

There are any number of expressions of this in scripture, but the seventh chapter of Romans brings it to focus. We hear Paul crying: "The good that I would I do not: but the evil which I would not, that I do. . . . O wretched man that I am! who shall deliver me?" (vv. 19, 24). That's the voice of a man bound by limitations. He makes resolutions; but he breaks them. He has aspirations; but he cannot realize them. Ideals flash; but he is not able to measure up. Longings surge in his soul; but he is frustrated with respect to them. He finds himself locked within limitations.

It is the limitation of weakness and death. A dead body attached is the image he uses. Death is ultimate weakness. A dead man has no strength to turn a finger!

This is what stirred the heart of Frederic W. H. Myers when he wrote:

> Oft when the word is on me to deliver
> Lifts the illusion and the truth lies bare;
> Desert or throng, the city or the river,
> Melts in a lucid paradise of air,—
> Only like souls I see the folk thereunder,
> Bound who should conquer, slaves who should
> be kings,
> Hearing their one hope with an empty wonder,
> Sadly contented in a show of things
> Then with a rush the intolerable craving
> Shivers through me like a trumpet-call,—
> Oh, to save these, to perish for their saving,
> Die for their life, be offered for them all!

Into this context of hopelessness and helplessness come Christ's evangels. Peter and John are on their way to the temple with the new sacrifice of praise. These two men, striding across the stage of life with a Spirit-infused gait, come upon a cripple. In this psychology of nonexpectancy that pervaded the life and in the midst of a religion that was as predictable as the setting of the sun, in this mood of quiet ennui, there is a mighty explosion of faith! Peter and John raise the level of expectancy. "He expected something of them."

The power of God will never get in the exercise of the will until it gets in the expectation of the hearers. Every situation is simply bursting with possibility if we can bring to bear the spiritual power of expectancy.

We first need to know what God expects of us. "For I know the thoughts that I think toward you, saith the Lord, thoughts of peace, and not of evil, to give you an expected end" (Jer. 29:11). We have resigned ourselves to a kind of fatalism that makes us little more than what someone has described as "an inert piece of chewing gum rolling around in the jaws of history." We insist on seeing ourselves as prisoners of our genes, our times, our circumstances. A friend said to me, "I am a born pessimist. I wake up in the morning, and even if it is a clear day, I am certain it is a weather breeder for a storm." We have all heard of that fatalist's epitaph, "I expected this and here I am." Someone has offered the premise that Adam took so long to die because he did not expect it. He had never seen death and had it in neither his consciousness nor his vocabulary.

The good news of the gospel liberates us from that sort of outlook. Even if the script of life has already been written, not one line of it contains a defeat clause. Listen to Psalm 139:16 in *The Living Bible:* "You saw me before I was born and scheduled each day of my life before I began to breathe. Every day was recorded in your Book!"

God's expected end for us is good, not evil. That is our predestination. Our election is another matter since that waits the movement of our will. When Jesus said, "Wilt thou be whole?" he was not addressing a concourse of traffic lights whose reaction was predetermined by the man who set the switch. What do you expect of God? What do you expect of yourself? Caleb, the man who, with Joshua, entered the Promised Land, was vigorous at eighty-five and said, "As yet I am as strong this day as I was in the day that Moses sent me: as my strength was then, even so is my strength now. . . . Now therefore give me this mountain, whereof the Lord spake in that day" (Josh. 14:11, 12).

The mountain Caleb wanted was Hebron. This was the most powerful stronghold of the enemy. It was guarded by awesome giants. Hebron meant fellowship, and Caleb was determined to have fellowship with God despite the obstacles.

"Hebron therefore became the inheritance of Caleb the son of Jephunneh, the Kenezite unto this day, because that he wholly followed the Lord God of Israel (Josh. 14:14).

> Joshua, the son of Nun,
> And Caleb, the son of Jephunnah,
> Were the only two
> Who ever got through
> To the land of milk and honey.

It is expectancy that keeps us alive and exhilarated. One saint, when asked about retirement, replied, "Full steam ahead till the boiler bursts!" There is a difference between getting old and growing old. We should never get old but grow on in expectancy. The course is forever. Whatever our age we have only a running start. We belong to a Kingdom that can stand everlasting increase.

A lecturer to young preachers advised: "Set goals for twenty years ahead in your churches. Plan to reach those goals. Don't be shortsighted. It is better to shoot at something and miss it than to shoot at nothing and hit it. Anyway, your successor can better alter your plans than to make order out of chaos."

Never make plans for failure and sickness. For if "where sin abounds there does the grace of God much more abound," it is also true that where there is sickness, health much more abounds. Where there is lack, prosperity much more abounds. Where there is loss, gain much more abounds, and where there is limitation, possibility much more abounds.

William Carey's formula has a sustained fascination to me: "Expect great things from God; attempt great things for God."

But we come to grips with the text when we ask, What do you expect of others? Peter and John could not meet this man on an economic level. They met him on a higher level. When will governments and churches realize that the most vital need of men is not such things as money or housing alone? We have all but destroyed the expectations of men by giving them such low benefits. What have we to give to this world? I mean beyond a few dollars and the meaningless patter of do-goodism that flings money carelessly in the lap of needs, dumps surplus on despondent circumstances, and dispenses charity from a heart unblessed and a head unbowed?

The deliverance this world needs will take a miracle. W. H. Auden has captured it in these lines:

> We who must die demand a miracle.
> How could the Eternal do a temporal act,
> The Infinite became a finite fact?
> Nothing can save us that is possible:
> We who must die demand a miracle.

Notice the ingredients of this miracle: it may be summed up in three words: the link, the lift, and the leap.

1. THE IMPORTANT LINK. Christians are God's functioning intermediaries between the world's limitations and God's unlimitedness. We are a kingdom of priests, God's bridge-builders.

A friend said he never understood the nature of our priesthood until one day in a desperate hour there walked into his small son's hospital room a man in priestly garb. He was presumptuously asking for the privilege of praying for this desperately ill lad. The illness had been diagnosed as incurable, and his life was held in the balance. The father had requested prayer among all his Christian acquaintances. But no sign of health appeared in the condition of the child. There entered the room that memorable day one who appeared to be a priest. The father's Protestant prejudice against clerical collars surfaced. But he was willing in that desperate hour for anyone to pray. I shall not forget how he shared the suprise of joy. "That dear man stood over my son's bed in priestly fashion," he said. "He began to pray and take authority. Then he said, 'Thomas, I bless you with health. I bless you with life. I bless you with healing. I bless you with joy and peace, in the name of the Father, and of the Son, and of the Holy Ghost.' The minister then turned and forthwith departed. From that moment my son showed signs of marked improvement; health and triumph over sickness."

But what followed is significant. He said: "I never knew what a priest was until that day. I had preened my Protestant feathers, thinking I could go directly to the throne of grace. I still believe that. But I learned that day that a true priest is one who has one hand on God and the other on our human need and allows the power to flow."

This is what Peter and John were doing. They were under the authority of their exalted Head, the risen, living Lord Jesus Christ. They were in touch with their throne rights. With the other hand they laid hold upon desperate human need, and the power came through. Most of us do not need a blessing quite as much as we need a ditching! Rufus Moseley used to say that there was no need to pray for a shower on a swamp.

In 1540 Martin Luther's good friend Frederick Myconius lay dying. Luther received a farewell letter from his friend, written with a weak and trembling hand. Immediately Luther sent back this reply: "I command thee in the name of God to live because I still have need of thee in the work of reforming the church. The Lord will not let me hear while I live that thou art dead, but will permit thee to survive me. For this I am praying. This is my will because it is God's will and may my will be done, because I seek only to glorify the name of God my Savior."

The dying man had already lost the power of speech when this letter arrived. But within a short time he was well again. He survived Luther by two months! Power came according to the word of faith. And power came to this poor lame man in the words of Peter. He did the impossible. Rise up and walk! That command was his enabler. The summons of the gospel contains the gift of grace. In response to God's "you can" we are enabled to say "I will!" When Jesus says, "Repent and believe" men suddenly find themselves able to do as he commands. The word he spoke was the bridge over which grace traveled to this weak and helpless man. There came to him the divine enablement, instinctive with life and joy and victory.

God not only restores our fellowship, he restores our humanity. For the true content of the human is the indwelling of the Divine. The preaching of the gospel is imperative. It is an offer of life. It energized this poor man and reversed the tragic history of forty years.

2. THE INSTANT LIFT. We need not stay weak

one moment longer. "And he took him by the right hand, and lifted him up: and immediately his feet and ankle bones received strength" (Acts 3:7). How we balk at this! We want to merge into the will of God imperceptibly. We want to be full but not filled; we want to grow into grace but never take the decisive step to enter the grace without which there can be no growth. Negotiating with God is like stepping off the ground and into an airplane. You have not arrived at your destination the moment you step onto the plane, not even at the moment it becomes airborne. But you have stepped out of a static relation with earth into a dynamic relation with the plane. There are those who are still sitting in the airport, thinking they have boarded the plane. And year after year they fail to experience the thrill and dynamic of that motivating grace of God that comes suddenly, like a mighty rushing wind.

Even growth begins suddenly. It begins when the seed goes into the ground. One doesn't put the seed in gradually. Then comes the day when new life springs forth. It is this thrust into a sudden realization of God that sets men on a new quest for holiness.

Look again at the Christian vocabulary. Against the background of indecisiveness, the Christians cut right through the confusion and indefiniteness of their time. Straightway! Immediately! At daybreak! Now!

> Savior, to Thee my soul looks up,
> My present Savior, Thou;

In all the confidence of hope
I claim the blessing now.
                                    Charles Wesley

3. THE IMPRESSIVE LEAP. "And he leaping
up, stood, and walked, and entered with them into
the temple" (Acts 3:8). I shall not attempt to tone
that down. There is no hint that they acted like
uncontrollable Holy Rollers. But let's not assume
that it was in anywise congruous with the "tame-
ness, sameness, and lameness" of our formal
church services. There was something of a fiery
abandon, an irrepressible gaiety of soul, a spon-
taneous outburst of holy joy.

Hear him, ye deaf; his praise, ye dumb,
    Your loosened tongues employ;
Ye blind, behold your Savior come;
    And leap, ye lame, for joy.
                                    Charles Wesley

They sing. They exhort. They exult in their new
life. The cold critic, outside this joyous group,
looks on with amazement and disdain. From the
standpoint of moral frigidity, the arctic belt of
unbelief, who shall say that the critic is not right?
But ask the man who has felt it. He will tell you it is
worth something to be so free.

W. E. Sangster, in that classic book on sanctity
The Pure in Heart, gives account of those who join
ranks with the overcomers, men and women who
have tasted living water bursting freshly from the
rock of faith. How they did storm the unbelieving
world with their sacrificial lives and their exuber-

ant song! They pierced the darkness with dawning light. One among them was a Salvationist. Dr. Sangster writes, "When Dr. Farmer, organist at Harrow, pleaded with the Salvationist drummer not to hit the drum so hard, the beaming bandsman replied: 'Lor' bless you, sir, since I've converted I'm so happy, I could bust the blooming drum!'"

I know there are those who would arch their brows and pour the acid of contempt on this kind of thing. But I don't mind telling you that the New Testament excites me!

The point, however, is not the demonstrative reaction of the healed enthusiast. The impressiveness of the miracle is the demonstration of a new adequacy at the point of his limitation. He was made masterful at the point of his greatest weakness.

They walk across the stage of life. They are men who were saddled with crippling disabilities and every conceivable disadvantage. John Clifford and his frail body; Alexander Whyte with the stigma of illegitimate birth; Henry Manning with the complete bankruptcy of his father's estate; Bud Robinson with his twisted tongue and untutored intellect; Curé of Ars and his fellow clerics' disdain—they all shout a defiance in the face of their limitations and herald down the centuries the adequacy of Christ!

There were those who were very critical of John Wesley. But Wesley knew the delivering power of grace. The Bishop of London attacked his methods. In a letter, he described them as being unconventional and vulgar. Wesley replied in these words:

> The habitual drunkard who was, is now temperate in all things, the immoral flee fornication. He that stole steals no more, but works with his hands; he that cursed and swore has now learned to serve the Lord with fear and rejoice with Him in reverence. He who was formerly a slave is now free.

And then he closes with this, "I can name these men and I can give you their places of abode." No one can gainsay such a witness! Loosed from themselves they are bound to him forever. They are only limited to his unlimitedness! Out from Nazareth this Evangel is sent to the limitless borders of mankind, "delivering those who are bound."

GOOD NEWS
TO THE BLIND

He hath sent me . . . to preach deliverance . . . ,
and recovering of sight to the blind.
Luke 4:18

═══════════════════════════════

BARTIMAEUS IS OUR NAME

Blind Bartimaeus . . . sat by the highway
side begging.
Mark 10:46

═══════════════════════════════

Jesus preached and the year of jubilee began. It
was a year of redemption and release for all who
would respond in faith to God's loving confrontation: "Repent: for the kingdom of heaven is at
hand."

But before men could see that Kingdom, they
had to have their eyes opened to reality. Jesus kept
repeating: "Except a man be born again, he cannot
see" (John 3:3); "Having eyes, *see* ye not?" (Mark
8:18); "Blessed are the eyes which *see* the things ye
see" (Luke 10:23).

Lack of sight brings depression and despon-
dence. That is the reason a blind man can so easily

106

catch our sympathy and relieve us of our coins. A blind man in Jesus' day was destined to be a beggar. His blindness robbed him of his social dignity and personal initiative and human potential. Jesus used this blindness to throw into bold relief the spiritual blindness of his contemporaries. That is the extraordinary thing about the Gospels—we want a comfortable place as a spectator, an onlooker. And suddenly we realize that we are not looking at these characters. We are, rather, looking with them. This is your life and mine.

The Son of man seemed especially pitying toward blindness. Indeed, as the Holy Spirit was sent to perpetuate his works, that ministry is associated more with perception than with power, more with vision than with vitality. It is the Holy Spirit who opens "the eyes of [our] understanding . . . ; that [we might] know what is the hope of his calling" (Eph. 1:18).

The "hope of his calling": the world in large segments is blind to it. The proof of it is the illusions we human creatures cherish, the prejudices we mistake for truths, the circumstances that we allow to depress us, the moral compromise that progressively stigmatizes our vision. We are drenched today with cynicism from our novelists, journalists, playwrights, music-makers, academicians, and policy-makers who have no clue as to God's purposes in history. Without God in their thoughts, they are simply—as Jesus put it—"the blind leading the blind." Democracy languishes.

For one hundred blind men cannot see any better than one. The blind man on the Jericho roadside is just ourselves, until God in Christ has opened our understanding.

I

In one of George Moore's novels he tells of those Irish peasants who came through the Great Depression. They were given work by the government. They built roads as an artificial stimulant to the economy. For a time they worked well, rejoicing that they were creatively employed again. They swung their picks and sang their Irish songs. But little by little they discovered that these roads were linked with no passageways, no further extensions. They simply ran out into dreary bogs and stopped. And as the truth gradually dawned on them that the roads were pointless, that they were working only to derive government help and to be fed, they grew listless. They leaned on their shovels, and their songs ceased.

When men no longer see any ultimate goal of life, no kingdom of God toward which the whole creation moves, then despair grips the heart. The will to live wanes. The song goes out of life. If the road leads only to a six-foot piece of real estate needing perpetual care, then what is the use of it all? People can stand anything as long as they know that what they are doing has ultimate significance, that the end spells fulfillment. Blindness to the kingdom of God relegates any

108

of us to the grind of poverty and the blight of depression.

We pity blindness. It is strange that we have no pity for deeper blindness, else would we not pity ourselves? There is an unmistakable connection between cynicism and blindness, between lack of divinely given insight and the mood of despair about the future. "Let us not be weary in well doing: for in due season we shall reap, if we faint not" (Gal. 6:9). And what will keep us from fainting? "I had fainted, unless I had believed to see the goodness of the Lord in the land of the living" (Ps. 27:13).

Men go quite well on the gusto of youth. A good set of glands can be a deceitful substitute for a good supply of grace. But high noon of life is no fixture. And that is the reason we begin to give up on ourselves and our world. Especially is this true in middle age. Do you know why it is called that—middle age? That is where our age begins to show up. It is when we get "thick and tired" of it all. One dear man slumped in his chair, totally discouraged, and sighed, "I am tired of it all—tired way down into the future."

But the thickness and tiredness is in our heads. John has an interesting commentary here: "And as Jesus passed by, he saw a man which was blind from his birth. And his disciples asked him, saying, Master, who did sin, this man, or his parents, that he was born blind? Jesus answered, Neither hath this man sinned, nor his parents: but that the works of God should be made manifest in him"

(9:1–3). Jesus saw this incident, not as something for speculation or judgment or something to lament. The rabbis had their rigid theory about such cases: every misfortune a direct punishment for individual or corporate wrongdoing. Jesus set all this aside as too crude and superficial to fit the facts. He rebuked his disciples for their theological wrangling. He thought it useless for them to attempt to surmise how the situation arose. Rather, seeing that the situation is here, how can we let God in on it now, so that his will takes control? The works of God can be manifested right here! Jesus could enunciate the good news of "the acceptable year of the Lord" in the midst of the most formidable circumstances. Any human situation can immediately become the receptacle by which the works of God can be exercised.

In other words, there are no irreparable disasters when faith takes charge. For faith releases God into the situation. "What shall we do, that we might work the works of God?" asked the disciples. Jesus shifted from the plural to the singular, "This is the work of God, that ye believe on him whom he hath sent" (John 6:28, 29). What is the work of God? It is simply God at work! Believe, said Jesus, and you will release God's work in human life.

II

Human life is beset with tragedy. Blindness is a devastating affliction. The Emperor Adrian accidentally shot a servant through the eyes with an arrow. He was filled with such remorse and pity that he offered the servant anything in his kingdom. The man could only say, "I wish I had my eyes." There was no sufficient cure or compensation.

This is why blindness raised the miracle of sight into such instructive prominence and desirable eminence. Jesus used it as a parable of our condition: "And see ye indeed, but perceive not" (Isa. 6:9), echoing the words of Jeremiah, "Which have eyes, and see not; which have ears, and hear not" (5:21).

Someone asked Helen Keller, "Isn't it terrible to be blind?" Miss Keller replied, "It is more terrible to have eyes and not see." One of the tragic things of modern life is the way in which our faculty of vision gets blurred and corroded. People walk the pathways of our existence with blind brows above empty hearts. Their sight never penetrates far enough to become insight.

We look but do not see. "Except ye become as little children, ye cannot see." The senses of wonder, innocence, and expectancy of childhood are captured in this experience of Russell Criddle's in his book *Love Is Not Blind.*

Following many years of blindness, a miraculous operation which grafted a new cornea on his eye enabled Mr. Criddle to see. When he was making his way home in New York, after the operation, he suddenly realized what it meant to have sight restored:

111

Everything looked beautiful. . . . There was the beauty of people. Some children were playing in the driveway. An old lady walked toward us, and passed. I felt no great thrill that I was no longer blind; only the awful sense of beauty thrilled me to the limit of endurance.

I hurried into the house and to my room and buried my head in the pillow. Not because I was no longer blind, not because I could see, but because I had not the capacity to digest so much grandeur. I wept. (W. W. Norton, p. 260)

What a fresh, wonderful spirit of discovery and human delight for living. A false ego blinds us to this; the lust of the flesh, the lust of the eyes, and the pride of life rob us of such grandeur. A jaded and jaundiced inner disposition will block out the light of the kingdom of God.

III

Blind Bartimaeus is the name of our civilization. A civilization that is largely blind to God's purposes that sweep history, to our true destiny, to who we are and why we are. Victor Frankl has said, "If a man has a *why* to live for he can bear almost any *how*." It is our interpretation of events, our insight, that is critical.

We wonder why sight is not given to us. We promise ourselves that after each war there shall be a new earth. We envision peace and prosperity for all men. We hope for a while, and then blunder down the same old blind and bloodstained pathways of the future. We beg for the bread of peace and are given the stones of despair.

Against this background of nihilism and determinism that has sabotaged the hopes and smothered the enthusiasm of this age is the good news that Jesus of Nazareth is passing by. Has the rumor ever reached you in the streets of life that there is a cure for inner darkness? We were not born to be blind toward eternity.

The background may be dark and dismal and desperate, but the God who came to Israel in exile, who was reconciling the world to himself in the grossness of Calvary, is not deserting the world that is stumbling through the shadows right now. Behind those shadows is the light of prophetic utterance, "And I will bring the blind by a way that they knew not; I will lead them in paths that they have not known" (Isa. 42:16). Jesus Christ is passing our way. And his passing is the fulfillment of that prophetic asseveration as he sends a shaft of light and a beam of hope into these faint hearts of ours.

THE MAGNETISM OF THE UNSEEN

And when he heard that it was Jesus of
Nazareth, he began to cry out, and say,
Jesus, thou son of David, have mercy on me.
Mark 10:47

Bartimaeus did not have eyes to see Jesus. But the
inarticulate cry of his heart is what every preacher
has impinging upon his soul as he stands to de-
clare the year of jubilee each Lord's Day. "Sirs, we
would see Jesus!" We dare not wrangle about
dead doctrine nor afflict precious moments with
humanistic surmisings nor engage in mock
crusades against positions we are sure will land us
on the side of public opinion, or at least with the
important minority. Our ordination is that men
may have their minds and hearts flooded with a
vision of the Son of God.

"Faith cometh by hearing, and hearing by the
word of God" (Rom. 10:17). It should be noted,

114

moreover, that when Mark refers to the rumor about Jesus' mighty ministry of deliverance, he is not sharing with us some isolated insight. The reference is repeated, underscored, flung up into instructive prominence. Here is a characteristic allusion: "He charged them that they should tell no man: but the more he charged them, so much the more a great deal they published it" (Mark 7:36).

Because of this, Bartimaeus had heard of Jesus. The rumors had reached him on the winds of chance that Jesus was coming his way. "And when he heard that it was Jesus of Nazareth, he began to cry out" (Mark 10:47). The very presence of Jesus incited expectancy. The unseen Savior magnetized his desire.

I

What had he heard that gave him such a basis for believing? He had certainly heard of the *ability* of Jesus. Doubtless the rumor had reached him of other blind men who had been healed. One such is recorded in Mark 8. Evidence was in abundance. G. K. Chesterton was inestimably right when he wrote: "The believers in miracles accept them because they have evidence for them. The disbelievers in miracles deny them because they have a doctrine against them." But every honest man must face the certainty that breaks the skepticism of every age, "Wherefore he is able."

He had heard of Jesus' *availability*. Jesus as God

with us! He comes at the call of help. He hears the faint cry. I was moved by the testimony of the driver of the tractor trailer who discovered that his brakes had given way as he started down an incline toward a major crossroads. He weaved in and out of traffic, crossing helter-skelter through intersections. Almost blind with fear, he finally brought the truck to a stop at the edge of an embankment.

He said that he instinctively turned to the Lord in prayer, crying out for help when these call letters came to him, "JE-333." Testifying of this extraordinary experience later, a friend said, "I didn't know God had a two-way-radio frequency." When he explained what he had in mind, it was a reference to Jeremiah 33:3, "Call unto me, and I will answer thee, and shew thee great and mighty things, which thou knowest not."

Mark tells us that Jesus, though on the mountain, saw those disciples wrestling with the turbulent sea. He knew where they were, why they were, and how they were. Has the good news of the availability of Jesus Christ for our needs penetrated your soul?

Bartimaeus heard of Jesus' *indispensability*. There was simply no one else on the field of life who could heal his blindness. Only because Christ is God, the Lord God Almighty who has wrapped around his uncreated deity our human flesh, can he have one foot in eternity and another in time so as to rescue us. "I find," said Augustine, "in my studies of Plato and Cicero many fine things acutely said, but in none of them did I find, 'Come unto me, and rest.' No, indeed, for that is Christ alone. Here is the true man who knows man and the true God who can redeem and rescue men." He stands as the only fulfilling alternative to the aimless desperation of our frustrated existence.

Bartimaeus heard of Jesus' *approachability*. He, Christ, is the Son of man. He can be sought.

We must be careful to define our terms. We speak of Jesus as a man like God. That is not sufficient. Jesus is not like God. God is like Jesus. He is all of God we can ever know and as much of God as we shall ever need. He is approachable. "Him that cometh to me I will in no wise cast out" (John 6:37). As Norman Snaith has put it, "God was from the beginning transcendent in that He was different from men, but He was by no means transcendent in that He was remote from men."

This was the basis of Bartimaeus' faith as he began to cry out. His action was really a reaction to Jesus' sovereign movement in history. When Jesus passes by, it is like the opening of a door which creates a concussion of air. Jesus creates a draft of faith that invigorates the languid soul.

II

Bartimaeus cried out, "Have mercy on me!" The only reason we can come to Christ is his mercy. Mercy is withheld judgment. "It is of the Lord's mercies that we are not consumed, because his compassions fail not. They are new every morning: great is thy faithfulness" (Lam. 3:22–23). Is it anything short of a miracle that history as we know it continues to this day? When we think of all the races of men who have gone their way across this earth, the contagion of their sin one after another, is it not a miracle that we have not long ago disappeared through irrecoverable corruption? When we think of all the Genghis Khans, Adolph Hitlers, and Joseph Stalins; when we think of the Eichmanns, Capones, and Dillingers; when we think of the John Smiths and Mary Joneses who have strutted and sinned their way across history, scattering the fallout of their pride and wickedness to the four winds, it must be the foremost conservation project of God that we are not consumed.

Judgment is what we deserve. In mercy God withholds that judgment. In grace he gives us abundantly in the face of what we do not deserve. Mercy is God's feeling toward us in the hurt of sin.

I wish the world knew this. Sometimes people refer sardonically to the hypocrites who go to church. But those of us who frequent the house of God do so not because of our self-righteousness but because of a consciousness of our sinnerhood. We are no better than anyone else or better than we want to be, just better than we used to be, thank God. The church is perhaps the only organization in the world that makes the requirement for entrance a sense of being unworthy to enter. It is not for those who feel they have achieved or that they merit something from God. Elton Trueblood suggests a new name for the church, "Sinners Anonymous." Yes, that's right. We are meant to be a society of the unworthy who have our sins forgiven and a new sense of worth put upon us. *Saints are but sinners who have cried out for sight!*

So Bartimaeus' coming was predicated upon the mercies of God: "Thou son of David, have mercy on me" (Mark 10:47).

"Jesus stood still, and commanded him to be called." Jesus stood still! God in the flesh is on an eternal errand, following a cosmic timetable to the Cross. He walks the dusty streets of Jericho, the city of roses. But it is not just moonlight and roses in Jericho. It is daylight and ditches! And out of the ditch of despair this poor man cries, and the Lord of the universe, the Creator of heaven and earth, stops to give his whole attention to a dirty beggar. That put identity and dignity upon that beggar far beyond human computation.

That speaks to us of the essential worth of the individual. None of us may be *worthy* of salvation, but in the estimate of the Son of God we are *worth* salvation. We might wonder at times if God is so busy running his cosmos and untangling international problems that he has little time for us. But the great Presider of the macrocosm also presides over the microcosm. He is sovereign over all.

I heard an interesting story from a friend who

was told that the National Biscuit Company was so well organized and supervised that they even had a vice-president in charge of fig newtons. He was so intrigued by this bit of information that he proceeded to investigate the truth of the allegation. So he called the switchboard receptionist and asked for the vice-president in charge of fig newtons. The reply he got blew his mind. The receptionist asked: "Is that packaged fig newtons or bulk fig newtons?" God is no less a particularist in the area of our human need.

This poor blind man in Mark's narrative was beginning to get his eyes opened to the mercies of a loving, caring God; so "he cried the more a great deal!" Nothing could stop the surge of his soul. Greater opposition only stirred him to greater entreaty.

"Be of good comfort, rise; he calleth thee" (Mark 10:49). He received the summons of heaven. The call of Christ in our hearts is more than an invitation. It is less than a coercion. It is a summons!

> Long my imprisoned spirit lay,
> Fast bound in sin and nature's night;
> Thine eye diffused a quickening ray;
> I woke, the dungeon flamed with light;
> My chains fell off, my heart was free,
> I rose, went forth, and followed thee.
> Charles Wesley

We do not come to accept Christ. We receive the revelation to the heart that we are accepted by Christ to come.

"And he, casting away his garment, rose, and

came to Jesus" (vs. 50). This was the long flowing garment he had worn to keep the heat off by day and the chill away by night. It was the only security he had. But in coming to Jesus he let go that security and clung to a greater. "We must throw off every encumbrance, every sin to which we cling, and run with resolution" (Heb. 12:1 NEB). "If you have really heard his voice and understood the truth that Jesus has taught you, . . . what you learned was to fling off the dirty clothes of the old way of living, which were rotted through and through with lust's illusions, and, . . . put on the clean fresh clothes of the new life which was made by God's design" (Eph. 4:22–24 Phillips).

He flung away the old securities and virtually leaped to Jesus. "And Jesus answered and said unto him, What wilt thou that I should do unto thee?" (Mark 10:51).

That seems like a very obvious question to put to this blind man. Or was it? Perhaps the Lord Jesus Christ was seeking to emphasize this very truth. "Do you understand the significance of the miracle that I want to perform, Bartimaeus? Is it simply that you want me to give you a cushion on which to sit, that you may beg in greater comfort? Or are you prepared to recognize the inevitable implications of having your eyes opened and your sight restored? For the moment I touch your eyes and you can see, you can beg no more. You will assume new responsibilities from which you cannot escape."

That is a sobering implication. Do we really

121

want to be whole? Do we want to be free from our insecurities and resentments and pride and peevishness and pusillanimous perspective?

When counseling the troubled we often discover that they have imbibed the lie of determinism. The first thing they usually want is a sympathetic ear. They want us to know of their suffering and greatly desire to elicit our empathy. When that is vouchsafed there is usually a curious turn. Then comes the strong case to convince us that the problem exists outside themselves. It is all in circumstances. It is all those inflexible people with whom they have to deal, or those intolerable circumstances.

If one were really logical about this, if this were true, their trouble would be compounded. For there is no guarantee that the "them" or the "it" out there is ever going to change. The only hope lies in a change in themselves.

Yes, Lord, this is what I desire. I do not want to go through life being a beggar, ekeing out a living by dependence on somebody else. I want to become a whole, responsible human being, purposeful, creative, and positive in my approach to life! "Lord, that I might receive my sight!" (vs. 51b). "And Jesus said unto him, Go thy way; thy faith hath made thee whole. And immediately he received his sight, and followed Jesus in the way" (vs. 52).

But Jesus was on the way to Jerusalem to die on a cross, to be rejected and despised of men and to find eternal glory in a self-surrender to the

Father's will. Be that as it may. That is where Bartimaeus was going also. Christian commitment is an attachment to the person of Jesus Christ that is revolutionary, complete, and exclusive. Once we are committed, Christ's life becomes our life; his enemies become our enemies; his ways become our ways; his Cross becomes our cross, and a thousand thanks—his future becomes our future!

Sholem Asch, in *The Nazarene*, shares a perception that is illuminative. A blind man mocks Jesus, all his miracles and teachings, even though Jesus would have healed him had he called on the Son of God. Jesus asks, "What shall it avail thee if thou art made seeing with thine eyes and thy heart remaineth blind?" Sholem Asch imagines Jesus leading the blind man back to his mat: "Thou blind one, stay among the blind!"

If that word seems incongruous with our conception of Jesus, it is perhaps because we have failed to see that Jesus is not only the Savior who offers much, but also the Lord who expects much of his followers. Even so, Lord, "Give what you command, and command what you will."

GOOD NEWS
TO THE BRUISED

He hath sent me . . . to set at liberty
them that are bruised.
Luke 4:18

═══════════════════════════════

THE THORN OF GOD'S PURPOSE
IN THE FLESH OF SATANTIC INTENTION

═══════════════════════════════

Circumstances and situations buffet, bruise, and
make life almost unbearable. Christ came to give a
new resource to the bruised, a transcendent over-
coming dimension of life.

Here is a category of human need that requires
careful delineation. We must see the difference
between the brokenhearted and the bruised.

In II Corinthians 11, we read the catalogue of
Paul's physical sufferings. For example, note
verses 23–24: "in labours more abundant, in
stripes above measure, in prisons more frequent,
in deaths oft. Of the Jews five times received I
forty stripes save one."

The Jews were not allowed to put a man to

124

death. It was only on extreme occasion that their wrath rose, and under the impulse of the moment, as in the case of Stephen's death, they vented lethal wrath. The death penalty could only be executed by the Romans. That was the reason Pilate had to be approached by the Jews before Jesus could be put to death. The Jews could only do what some considered a penalty worse than death. Using a multilashed whip, with bone and iron built into the ends of each lash, they could stripe a man. Coming down with that heavy whip on the victim's back, each blow would be multi-striped. Each extraction of the whip would pull flesh with it. It was a horrendous experience fraught with excruciating pain.

Paul says, "Of the Jews received I forty stripes save one." Thirty-nine stripes from a multitailed whip! And with bone, iron, and lead set in it. Think of the many lashes that wrapped him round and pulled away the flesh. This was the ultimate the Jews could give. Five times he received maximum punishment! Five times thirty-nine is two hundred less five, or one hundred ninety-five stripes, and multiple stripes at that.

That was what Paul endured! And much more. Three times he was beaten with rods (v. 25). The assailant would strike the back with a rod, across the spine. Anyone with back trouble might readily sympathize with Paul. That was enduring physical suffering!

Once he was stoned, shipwrecked three times, in watchings often (that is, sleepless nights).

These were extraordinary sufferings, fearful in nature. But so far as we can ascertain, all those scars on his back were healed. Paul believed in physical healing. He believed in the restoration of the body in strength and stamina. There is no doubt about it. God is on the side of healing. "He healeth all our diseases." Even if this reference in Psalm 103 is to soul diseases, we still know that God has put enough reserve in the human body to keep it going in health. When the Holy Spirit quickens the mortal body, it can be renewed in remarkable recovery.

Someone demurs and points to an old aunt who was a godly and praying woman but who died of some dreadful disease. That is irrelevant! An explanation is not always forthcoming for these cases. But what we do know is that God wills to heal. However, it is important that we understand that healing is not a moral issue. It is not a sin to be sick. Sickness does not break fellowship with God. Where a moral issue is involved, repentance can bring immediate forgiveness and restoration. But where there is no moral issue there can be a *time factor,* and the Resurrection is the final answer to our prayers for healing.

The total man is included in our redemption. There was total healing of the cosmos provided for in the Atonement. The minimum of the Atonement covered more than the maximum of the Fall. The healing of the whole earth is included in Christ's finished work. But there is a sovereign outworking. God is on the side of healing, healing for the body, for the environment, for the nations. So Paul, by faith, appropriated healing.

There is another picture presented in chapter 12:

> And lest I should be exalted above measure through the abundance of the revelations, there was given to me a thorn in the flesh, the messenger of Satan to buffet me, lest I should be exalted above measure. For this thing I besought the Lord thrice, that it might depart from me. And he said unto me, My grace is sufficient for thee: for my strength is made perfect in weakness. (vv. 7–10)

"There was given to me a thorn in the flesh, the messenger of Satan to bruise me." (*Bruise* and *buffet* are the same words in the Greek.) Paul was healed of his wounds but not healed of his bruises. He was healed of his stripes but given "liberty" over his bruises.

This phrase *thorn in the flesh* appears in the Bible many times. Our blessed Lord wore a crown of thorns. But in the original language the word is *akantha*. You may be familiar with the thorns of the pyracantha (*pyr-akantha*) shrub. But the word for thorn is not *akantha* in this context. Rather the word used here is *skolop* which means "stake." We all know the purpose of a stake. We drive it into the ground so that our trees might grow straight. It is not driven into the tree. It is driven into the ground in order to confine that tree. It shuts it up to one narrow purpose. Tomatoes are staked so they won't run all over the place but that they might grow in one direction. It is a stake that is driven in that prevents us from doing what we want to do and forces us to conform to a higher purpose. This is not removed, because it is used to keep us straight on the line of God's intention.

For some of us it is there all the time. It is not a little thing. It is a big thing. It limits us. It seems to hamper us. We can't get around as freely as we would like. It bruises us. "I besought God thrice," Paul said. And God said, "No, I am not going to heal you from this. I am going to give you a glorious liberty in it."

Paul cried to be healed. Did he deserve it? Yes. Were Paul's prayers prayers of faith? Yes. Did he deserve to have his prayers answered? Yes! A thousand times yes! He agonized with God three times. "Lord," he said, "this thing limits me, take it out of the way." But God said, "Paul, it is to you a *problem*. It is for me a *plan*."

Do you know what it is to be limited? Limited to the degree that you feel you cannot have the full expression of your vocational calling? Limited as a mother, as a wife, as a husband, as a son, or as a daughter? "These things bruise," says Paul.

A bruise comes, and then usually rot and decay follow. Watch it in an apple or melon. An apple is bruised through mishandling, and that bruise invites decay. That's what happens in fruit. But the great tragedy is in human lives. Many a lost soul today is the result of bruising. A careless jostling of a child. I see them every week of my ministry. I've seen wives bruised by husbands and husbands by wives. I've seen children bruised by callous parents. There is a deep hurt. I've seen good people bruised by cunning and malicious treatment.

Joseph knew what it meant to be bruised. Taken maliciously by his brothers when still a young man, he was sold into slavery. Rising to prominence in Potiphar's house, he was lied about by his master's wife and put into prison. He did not deserve to be there. He was a bruised boy. An ordinary young man could have gone bad in those circumstances. He could have said, "Life is a tale told by an idiot, full of sound and fury." He could have said, "The time is out of joint, O cursed spite, that I was ever born to set it right!" He could have said, "Life is a long fool's errand to the grave."

God allowed Satan to drive that stake, and it kept Joseph on the line of God's greater intention. Finally, there was corn in Egypt when a civilization was in hunger. The corn was there because Joseph was there. Joseph was there because God gave him liberty in those circumstances. This ultimately drew his father and brothers to Egypt resulting in their salvation.

The injustice of it all must have hurt Joseph more than the handcuffs and leg-irons of the prison.

Consider the children of our generation. Homes are running out of love. The flame of marital commitment flickers and dies. Innocent little ones are caught in the crossfire of resentments, accusations, and legal proceedings. Fearful hearts, they are, whose moorings are insecure. Will they just drift and doubt and despair? Will they recover or carry those bruises which will cause rot and deterioration of the human spirit?

Many are carrying bruises today, hurts on the inside. If one is cut on the outside, he bleeds and everybody sees it. But when the bruise takes place inwardly, he smarts and feels the injustice of it all! Were you ever the subject of a piece of unwarranted gossip, some idle tale that reached you in its fifth repetition? And while it was going through it was being embroidered all the way along. When it reached you your response might have been, "Oh, that hurts! It's so unkind, so untrue!" You carried that bruise on the inside.

So the ministry of Christ is to deliver the bruised. One does not have to be a first rate artist to know that it is essential to a good picture that there should be shadows in it as well as light. Bach and Beethoven would understand how a discord could add excitement and beauty to harmony. "My temptations," said Luther, "have been my Master's in Divinity."

William James commented on that famous painting in the Bibliotheque Nationale, Paris, where Michael the Archangel is depicted with his foot on the neck of the devil. Upon reflection he said, "You know, I believe this world is all the richer for having a devil in it, if we can only keep our foot on his neck."

That's the question: Can we do it? There is a story about the fishermen off the coast of Labrador. They discovered a secret of preserving fish. This was back in the days before refrigeration, and the fish were kept alive in the deep wells of the ship. One man's fish were always firm and fresh. He got a better market price than his fellows. One day he died, and when a friend went into his ship he discovered a big horny-headed catfish in the well. That old catfish, although he ate a few fish, kept the other fish stirring and moving, on the alert, fighting for their lives.

It is great insight to be able to see the devil as God's catfish in the world's ship. He stirs the waters and makes those intent on serving God find a more powerful incentive for staying spiritually vigilant and vigorously alive.

It appears that the devil is fighting against the Great Design. He is literally kicking against the goad. In attempting to thwart God's purposes he bruises us. But in so doing he is making a colossal blunder, and God is making capital of it. If we read the Scriptures with divine light above our eyes, we could hardly miss Paul's meaning.

"My thorn in the flesh," says Paul, "is a messenger of Satan to bruise me." I think we need to score this point. Paul's thorn was an *angelos*, "a messenger of Satan." Most commentators of Scripture through the years have made this "thorn in the flesh" refer to a physical disability. A few have made it to be a strong uprising of concupiscence. But most commentators agree that Paul was impaled on some kind of trial. One suggestion is that it was malaria. Two of his companions left the malarial country. Tertullian intimated it was epilepsy. Another plausible explanation is that it was a handicap of the eyes. Paul makes reference to his physical appearance, even to suggesting that he might be repulsive to some. To the Galatians he wrote, "You would have plucked out your eyes for me." Others contend that it was that bright light on the Damascus road that affected his sight thereafter. One dear old lady in Sunday school commented, "And that fall off the horse didn't do him any good either!" In any case, he was blind for several days afterward.

I would not contend for any one interpretation. Obviously, it is not essential that we know. It does not seem tenable that a man with such a debilitating physical infirmity could possibly have withstood the pressures and privations, the hazards, hardships, and heroisms that characterized his battered and besieged life. Had Paul been saddled with all the diseases and infirmities that men have attributed to "the thorn in the flesh," he would have been dead with consumption long before he launched his missionary campaigns.

We can speculate endlessly. It was a *skolop* that Satan inflicted but which God used, whether it was a physical infirmity, the trials of life, or a special burden. Satan used it to hamper and hinder. God used it to prosper and further.

Jesus came to preach deliverance to the bruised. It was said of Jesus that, Son though he was, "he learned obedience by the things which he suffered." The problem of evil and suffering is raised

132

far more by the spectator than by those who are the actual combatants in life. People outside the Christian commitment say, "How can God allow that and be good?" But those in the battle find treasures in darkness. The skeptic is not the one in the battle. He is on the sideline calling the fouls of the game, judging God. It is precisely the world's great sufferers who manifest an unconquerable faith that triumphs!

Who are those whose names stud the dramatic roll of the faithful in Hebrews 11:37–38? These are not men whose paths were primrose, who lived through circumstances that were sunny, serene, and sublime. The sun was not always shining, and the skies were not always azure. No! They were "stoned, sawn asunder, tempted, slain with the sword, destitute, afflicted, tormented, wanderers in deserts and mountains and dens and caves of the earth." But they came into the glory world, waving their report cards, "and they obtained a good report!" (v. 39) They graduated magna cum laude! Most of us graduate "Laude, how cum!"

It is not difficult to find those half-defeated and totally frustrated people who join the ranks of a sad proportion of our population. Their hope of happy living is choked off by the refrain, "I can't." "I can't face life with this liability." "I can't forgive." "I can't live without worry." There is only one answer. It is useless to talk to these people about the triumphant providences of God or the creative function of trouble or the philosophical nature of disappointment. That's nonsense. People do not need an explanation for the trouble that engulfs them. What's needed is a power to transcend it, to conquer *in* it. There has to come an endowment of inward liberty, the quickening of a steadfast hope, the confirmation of a pledged love. That is precisely what was given to Paul as expressed in these words: "My grace is sufficient for thee."

GRASPING THE NETTLE
AND EXTRACTING THE NECTAR

The gospel to the bruised is summed up in Paul's statement in II Corinthians 12:9–10: "And he [Christ] said unto me, My grace is sufficient for thee: for my strength is made perfect in weakness. Most gladly therefore will I rather glory in my infirmities, that the power of Christ may rest upon me. . . . For when I am weak, then am I strong."

Our concern is to explore the meaning of "my grace is sufficient for thee." The word *grace* is as essential to the Christian perception of existence as any word we use. It is a fundamental conception of God as a benevolent God and life as a positive affirmation. Behind all the meanness, badness, insanity, bloodshed, bodies ripped to shreds, wars, hijackings and Watergates, we would think this world was run by demons. However, God's grace overreaches our bad choices. Grace abounds much more than sin abounds. This simply means that though life appears to beat us and gouge us and rob us, yet ultimately life has more to give than it has to take. It is a way of saying that the arms of the universe are stretched out, not to crush us but to embrace us, not to extinguish us but to extend us. *Grace* is a distinctive word. It is different from *justice*. Justice is what we deserve. Knowing the sin of the human heart, the antagonism of that heart toward God, the rebellious nature of the human will—knowing all this, whatever we received of punishment would be deserved. But grace is also distinctive from mercy. Grace is the life of God among men, overreaching his bad choices and human liabilities and finding a way to redeem. "My grace is sufficient for thee."

This is good news for the bruised. It means:
(1) THAT GOD IS IN THE BATTLE OF LIFE WITH US. He is not a detached spectator. In every pang that rent the heart of Paul, God was divinely aware. He had worn the flesh of man and tested its frailty.

See it in the book of Daniel. When Shadrach, Meshach, and Abednego had been flung into the furnace, not having been delivered from the actual circumstance of the fiery testing, some must have doubted. Multitudes might have come to gloat

136

over the extermination and the passing away of this ransomed remnant. Then transpired the truth that we face in Paul's great affirmation: "His grace is sufficient."

"Look," cried the king, his heart gripped with a glimpse of the supernatural, "did we not cast three men into the furnace? Why are there four? And the fourth is like the Son of God" (see Dan. 3:24–25).

Standing on this side of the Resurrection the answer rings with a triumphant certainty, "Who shall separate us from the love of Christ? shall tribulation, or distress, or persecution, or famine, or nakedness, or peril, or sword? . . . Nay, in all these things we are more than conquerors through him that loved us" (Rom. 8:35, 37).

A dear friend was relating this experience. He was quizzing his young son about the content of his Sunday school lesson. The response was given with the average nonchalance of a dispassionate pupil. "Ah," the boy said, "it was all about three men who fell into the fire." "But," persisted the father, "God helped them out, didn't he?" "Naw," the boy replied, "he fell in too!"

What a profound interpretation. The Word of the gospel is that God has fallen into our human dilemma with us. Wherever we are suffering, he is identified with us and is there to release the power of his resurrection.

James Gilmour, toward the end of his career as a pioneer missionary in Asia, wrote a letter home in which he said: "When I was a youth in Scotland I thought I heard a voice saying to me, 'James Gilmour, go to China.' I went to China. After a while I thought I heard a voice say to me, 'James Gilmour, go to Mongolia.' I discovered my misapprehension. Jesus Christ didn't say to me, 'Go to China.' What he said to me was, 'Come to China;' and when the other call came he did not say, 'Go to Mongolia,' but 'Come to Mongolia.' I found Him already there waiting for me when I arrived."

(2) THAT GOD IS NOT ONLY IN THIS WITH US, BUT WE ARE IN IT WITH HIM, sharing his redemptive activity. Because we *are* related to Christ, it is a foregone conclusion that we shall suffer. "All that will live godly in Christ Jesus shall suffer persecution" (II Tim. 3:12).

There is a scripture in the Epistle to the Colossians that I have always found difficult. It is apparently difficult for many commentators. They won't attempt to explain it. When they get to his verse they seem to gloss over it and go on to the next passage. I speak of Colossians 1:23*b*–24: "I Paul am made a minister; who now rejoice in my sufferings for you, and fill up that which is behind of the afflictions of Christ in my flesh for his body's sake, which is the church."

I don't know how to explain that. But, I am confident that it does not mean that there is anything deficient in the sufferings of Christ at Calvary. When Christ said, "It is finished!" there was a completed divine transaction. "It is finished" can in no wise have meant "I am finished."

So that is a settled matter. But one thing it must

mean. That Christ did not suffer all that God intended suffering to accomplish. This has to be made up in the Body of Christ, the church, under the test of time.

"There hath no temptation taken you but such as is common to man; but God is faithful, who will not suffer you to be tempted [buffeted, tried, bruised] above that ye are able; but will with the temptation also make a way of escape, that ye may be able to bear it" (I Cor. 10:13).

We cannot help capturing the sense of this in Jesus as he approached the Cross. Bruised, maligned, unjustly judged, lawlessly libeled, the Rose of Sharon crushed so cruelly beneath the beggar's heel was he. Calvary is faith's incredible way of grasping the nettle and extracting the nectar from it. Not the tragic event, but the turning of that event into something other than tragedy. This is the victory.

The greatest victories have been achieved by the army of the bruised. They were handed excellent excuses to commit suicide, drown themselves in day-dreams, deaden their sense of defeat with drugs, take refuge in neuroses. But they refused to become the whining and whimpering mass of inferiority that they might have been. They came through—and came through victoriously—because they allowed the bruising to be the means of the release of the power of his resurrection. They were brought into the fellowship of his suffering, and they went through the "gates of splendor."

When we arrive at the book of Revelation we are told that those gates through which the victorious entered were "gates of pearl." William E. Sangster has an interesting account of the origin of the pearl. Pearls are a product of pain, he tells us. The shell of the oyster or mussel gets pierced, chipped, or perforated, and some alien substance (speck of sand) gets inside. Pearls are now made commercially this way. A speck of sand is deposited in the soft flesh, and it is irritated. Oysters haven't any hands. They have no defense. Things come into our lives, and we have nothing with which to fight back. A pearl begins with a pain.

But what does the oyster do? God has put in that oyster a substance. He exudes a pearl-like secretion that covers that irritant. The more the foreign matter irritates, the more the secretion covers. After a while, when the oyster matures; there is a full-grown pearl. Pearls are synonymous with ballroom gaiety. They are worn by people who want to forget that life has its somber and saddening side.

But pearls are not so made. They are made through suffering. What, then, is a pearl? *A pearl is nothing more than suffering covered by the provision of Almighty God.* That is the discovery Paul made through his "thorn in flesh." Suffering covered by the sufficiency of Christ. The tragic element of life transformed by divine agency!

The Gentiles were evangelized by an apostle with a stake in his flesh. Luke witnessed this firsthand as he wrote that remarkable account in the Acts of the apostles.

This triumphant spirit runs like a mighty river throughout the Bible. Its healing stream flows throughout church history. Cast one man into prison and he sulks and feeds on revenge and hardens. Cast John Bunyan into jail and he will write an immortal *Pilgrim's Progress*! Turn the lustrous bright eyes of one woman into milk-colored, sightless orbs, and she will forever curse the day of her birth. But let Fanny Crosby grasp that darkness and put the light of Christ over it, and she will set the world singing to the tune of her enraptured heart.

Strip one man of his wealth, and he will go crashing through the skylights and splash on the pavement below. But let it happen to a man named Job, and he will shout down the ages: "I know that my Redeemer liveth, and when He has tried me I shall come forth as gold."

Rob some men of their most tantalizing hope of marriage, and they will turn sour and cynical. But let it happen to Henry Martyn, and pain-drenched but triumphant he will fling that disappointment back into the face of the enemy, allowing the creativity of Christ to be magnified through him in prodigious missionary labors.

I believe Satan desires that the old sinful nature might express itself, that it be stimulated and aroused into sinful action when the testing comes. He wants to use it to incite us in rebellion against God. That is why it is called "Satan's messenger"!

All the devil succeeded in doing with Paul was driving him to a new depth of trust and obedient faith. He proved that the pressure of that thorn and the power of Calvary are completely bound up together.

The only road between a manger crib and a coronation turns through a garden gory with crimson sweat and over a mountain whose reeling summit is storm-scarred and cross-crowned. To detour here is to cancel arrival there. There is no shortcut! There is no bypass!

Jesus came to set at liberty the bruised. Satan wants to distort our thinking and bring despair. God wants to sanctify it and bring deliverance. The messenger of Satan was designed to overthrow Paul. But it was seized by the hand of faith and turned into a weapon to overthrow Satan. Among the last words of Romans is written this mighty affirmation, "And the God of peace shall bruise Satan under your feet shortly" (16:20).

The church's bruising became a weapon in their hands. These Christ-whelmed and grace-thrilled sons and daughters of the Lord God Almighty gave Satan one of the most monumental defeats of his ignominious career. Satan was a fool to buffet Paul. Would to God that through the same triumph of faith and the sufficiency of grace we might likewise trample under our feet the enemy of our souls.